Favorite
Desserts
Made
Gluten Free

Taste as Good as
The Real Thing

BY NOTED AUTHOR

AMELIA E. POHL

EAGLE PUBLISHING COMPANY OF BOCA

The following manufacturers and names appearing in this recipe book are registered names or trademarks:

Baker's Semi-Sweet Baking Squares
Baker's White Chocolate Baking Squares

Bob's Red Mill®	*Chefmaster®*
Crisco®	*Egg Beaters®*
Egg Replacer™	*Ener-G® Foods, Inc.*
Fig Newton®	*Grandma's® Molasses*
Hefty®	*Hershey's®*
Hostess Cupcake®	*Jello®*
Jet-Puffed Marshmallow Cream	*Just Whites®*
Karo®	*Kellogg's®*
King Arthur Flour	*Knox®*
Kraft®	*Lactaid®*
Lorna Doone®	*Marshmallow Fluff®*
Minute Tapioca	*Moon Pie®*
Nabisco®	*Oreo®*
Sno Ball®	*Sun Maid®*
Tastykake®	*Twinkie®*
Whole Foods, Inc.	*Williams-Sonoma®*

EAGLE PUBLISHING COMPANY OF BOCA
4199 N. Dixie Highway, #2
Boca Raton, FL 33431   E-mail: info@eaglepublishing.com

Printed in the United States of America
ISBN 1-932464-29-8   ISBN 9781932464290
Library of Congress Control Number: 2010934441

FAVORITE DESSERTS MADE GLUTEN FREE

Table of Contents

ABOUT THE AUTHOR

Before becoming an attorney in 1985, AMELIA E. POHL taught mathematics on both the high school and college level. During her tenure as Associate Professor of Mathematics at Prince George's Community College in Maryland, she wrote several books in the field of mathematics. As an attorney, Ms. Pohl combined her skills as teacher, author and lawyer, to write legal books for the general public. She wrote a series of legal books covering topics of estate planning, probate and guardianship.

Amelia Pohl's avocation, throughout her varied career was, and is, cooking. Beginning as a child with her first attempt (chocolate pudding made from a package) she collected and worked her way through countless cook books, always enjoying the challenge of trying to achieve the perfect cookie, cake, pie — the perfect meal. When her husband was diagnosed with Celiac disease, the challenge increased tenfold. It took her years of research and experimentation to prepare gluten free meals and desserts with the same results as their favorite wheat based dishes. She shares that knowledge in this the first of a series of three gluten free cook books that she has written.

ACKNOWLEDGMENT

I've written many books over the years. None so labor intensive as this one. I first had to research ways to make a popular dessert. Next I needed to adapt that recipe to the gluten free diet. Once I thought the recipe might work, I made it to see if it looked, tasted, and had the same texture as the original favorite. More often than not, it didn't and I had to start over again. It took me an average of four tries per recipe to get it right.

Of all the books and web sites I researched, the gluten free cook books of the late Bette Hagman were the most helpful. Bette was a pioneer, paving the way for gluten free cooking. Without her books, later cooks would have had to reinvent the "gluten free wheel."

This book was ten years in the writing. Without Bette to lead the way, it would have taken twenty.

THE RFT

This book is divided into two parts. The first part contains recipes of classic desserts baked at home: butter cookies, chocolate cake, apple pie, etc. The second part contains recipes of desserts sold commercially: 'Twinkies", "Moon Pies", "Hostess Cupcakes", etc. I put quotes around the name because the recipes are not those of the commercial favorites. They are gluten free recipes I invented so those who are unable to eat gluten can once again enjoy these classic favorites. Although not the original, each recipe qualifies as a RFT (Reasonable Facsimile Thereof).

FOREWORD

Having a doctor tell that you can't eat gluten is similar to a grieving process. First there is disbelief:
"How can I be allergic to wheat? I've eaten it all my life."

Next there is denial:
"Everyone knows how whole wheat is good for you. Can't be that it is poisoning my gut."

Then there is anger:
"You mean I can never eat cakes, cookies and pies? What's the point of living?"

Some time later there is acceptance:
"A gluten free diet is for life. Cheating is no good. I'm only hurting myself. I need to forget about my favorite desserts. I've got to learn to live without gluten."

Hopefully you are at the acceptance stage and are now ready to live without gluten. But there is no reason to live without your favorite desserts. You may not be able to buy them at the store, but you can make them at home, gluten free, using the recipes in this book. Your home baked favorite will taste just as good as "the real thing." In many cases, better.

The skeptic may be thinking, "There's got to be a catch . . . some downside." And there is. Baking takes time. If you have a full time job, you may need to do your baking on weekends, freeze the dessert and defrost it when you have the urge for something sweet. And learning how to bake gluten free could be another downer depending upon whether you are an enthusiastic learner or an intellectual couch potato.

Being a teacher and author, I wrote this book as I would any text book going from easy to "challenging" (modern word for "really hard") and all at a comfortable pace. The first lesson is a discussion of the different grains that can be substituted for wheat flour.

WHEAT SUBSTITUTE

There are many different flours that can be substituted for wheat flour. They have unfamiliar names, but when properly blended, look and taste like wheat flour. I developed two gluten free blends, one to replace all purpose wheat flour and the other a gluten free cake flour blend. Both start with a basic gluten free blend.

BASIC GLUTEN FREE (G-F) BLEND
2 PARTS WHITE RICE FLOUR
2 PARTS TAPIOCA FLOUR
1 PART SORGHUM FLOUR
1 PART POTATO STARCH

One part Garbanzo & Fava flour is added to the basic blend to make a G-F ALL PURPOSE FLOUR. One part corn starch is added to the basic blend to make a G-F CAKE FLOUR. With these blends replacing wheat flour, I was able to reproduce all of the desserts I so enjoy.

Finding the right combination of grains was one problem solved. Measuring out five different flours to make a pie or cookie was another problem. The solution was simple enough. Prepare a large container of each gluten free flour in advance and then measure the flour out as needed. Page 198 of the Appendix explains how to prepare and store these two gluten free blends.

THE COMMERCIAL ALL PURPOSE BLEND

There was no gluten free blend on the market when I started my gluten free diet. Today there are several gluten free all purpose flours on the market. You may want to use a commercial blend rather than take the time to mix your own. All purpose G-F flour blends are readily available at Whole Foods, Inc., health food stores and over the Internet.

One drawback to using a commercial gluten free blend is uniformity company to company. All purpose wheat flour looks, tastes and bakes the same no matter which company produces the flour. Not so with G-F all purpose flours. Different companies use different blends of ingredients. In one blend, the primary ingredient is Garbanzo Bean Flour. In another, it is Brown Rice Flour. They are sold in small quantities, so it is easy and inexpensive to try different brands until you find the one that works best for you.

NO COMMERCIAL G-F CAKE BLEND

Most of the recipes in this book use G-F All Purpose Flour. The more delicate cakes need the light G-F Cake Flour. There is no commercially prepared gluten free cake flour on the market at this time. Substituting a commercial G-F all purpose blend for G-F Cake Flour blend may not give you the same taste or texture. To get the best results for the recipes in this book calling for G-F Cake Flour, mix a batch of Gluten Free Cake Flour using the recipe on page 198.

XANTHAN GUM

Substituting a blend of different flours for wheat flour is not the whole story when it comes to gluten free baking. Gluten is the substance found in wheat that "glues" things together. Xanthan Gum replaces the gluten found in wheat based flours. It is produced by Bob's Red Mill and sold at Whole Foods, Inc. The amount of Xanthan Gum per recipe is small. In general, it is a half a teaspoon of Xanthan Gum per cup of flour for cakes and cookies. See the GLOSSARY for an explanation of this and other gluten free ingredients.

LEAVENING

Solving the problem of "glue" is relatively easy, compared to the problem of density. Gluten free blends are more dense than wheat flour. If you try to substitute a G-F blend for wheat flour in your favorite cake recipe, you will probably be disappointed. It is necessary to add special leavening agents to the G-F blend to overcome the problem of baked goods that do not rise properly. Gluten free recipes utilize the usual leavening agents: yeast, eggs, baking soda, baking powder. Many recipes need additional help with things such as Egg Replacer (an egg substitute) or finely ground powdered milk.

THAT'S A LOT OF INGREDIENTS

Baking gluten free made me appreciate flour made from wheat. It takes a lot of ingredients to replace wheat flour. Happily, the method used to bake gluten free pies cookies and cakes is the same as that of wheat based flour. If you are an experienced cook, you can make desserts the same way as always — only with gluten free ingredients.

COULD BE LOTS OF FUN

You may think it tough luck to be saddled with an inability to digest gluten. But every downside has an upside. This could be an opportunity for exploring your creative side — a time for adventure. Do not be afraid to experiment. At worst, your garbage disposal will enjoy the feast. More likely, your mistakes will be minor ones. A bit too soft or crunchy, a little over or under cooked. All still edible, with a lesson to be learned for the next time. And when you get it right, you might experience something you never imagined — food ecstacy!

COUNTING CALORIES

I didn't. I know other recipe books indicate the number of calories, carbohydrate, fats and sodium (salt). I tried to follow the trend and quickly got discouraged. Many recipes in this book allow for substitutions. Grams of fat and salt vary depending on whether butter or margarine is used. Milk is another problem. Many recipes just say MILK, giving the reader the option of 1% fat, 2% fat, no fat, soy milk, Lactaid milk, etc. Calories, fat and salt content are very different from one milk to another. I came to the conclusion that giving numbers could only be an estimate. It would be misleading to those who are serious about keeping count to print numbers that are not accurate.

What I did do, was keep the sugar and fat content as low as possible without compromising the taste of the original favorite treat. The calorie/carbohydrate watcher can limit himself to a small portion and freeze the rest for a later time when diet permits.

About This Book

The format of this book is designed to assist the reader in making the recipe. Each recipe gives the ingredients in the order used. As mentioned earlier, sections of the book go from easy (Cookies) to "challenging" (Bakery Favorites).

BEGINNER FRIENDLY

Making a gluten free dessert may not be hard for an experienced cook, but for the occasional cook it may seem daunting. To help those new to baking, each section of the book begins with a "how to" page:

HOW TO MAKE DROP COOKIES

HOW TO MAKE REFRIGERATOR COOKIES, etc.

followed by recipes with just the ingredients.

The HOW TO section of the APPENDIX explains basic terms used within the recipes such as:

sift and mix

line the pan with parchment

cream shortening

cut in shortening

fold in beaten whites

make lemon rind

clarify butter

temper eggs

ALSO FOR THE EXPERIENCED

Experienced bakers will appreciate the format of directions on the beginning page and just the ingredients after that. Other books give the same directions for each recipe. Why read through the directions over and over again when all you want are the ingredients?

About This Book

THE INDEX

This book has an INDEX and an INGREDIENT INDEX. The Ingredient Index is something I wish was included in all cook books. Many times I have something left over and want to use it in a recipe. The Ingredient Index identifies recipes containing that item. For example, I might have left over cottage cheese. With the Ingredient Index I find that the recipe on page 23 (Lemon Drop Cookies) uses cottage cheese.

INGREDIENTS

For sake of brevity, I do not go into details as to the ingredient used in a particular recipe. For example, recipes that contain a spice such as CINNAMON, do not say GROUND CINNAMON, the "ground" being understood.

If you have any question about what to use in a given recipe, consult the following list of ingredients.

RECIPE INGREDIENTS

ALMOND MEAL means *finely ground almonds*. BOB'S RED MILL sells it as ALMOND MEAL/FLOUR.

BAKING COCOA means original unsweetened cocoa used for baking, such as HERSHEY'S COCOA.

BUTTER means *unsalted sticks of butter* (not whipped).

BUTTERMILK means *whole Buttermilk* or *1.5% fat.*

BROWN SUGAR means *packed* light or dark brown sugar.

COFFEE GRANULES means *instant coffee*.

RECIPE INGREDIENTS

COOKING SPRAY means *a gluten free, unflavored, vegetable spray.*

CORN SYRUP is available either as dark, or light (clear). It is sold under the brand name of KARO.

CRISCO is the brand name used for *unflavored vegetable shortening.*

DRIED EGG WHITES means *dehydrated egg whites.* It is sold under the brand name of JUST WHITES.

DRY MILK means *instant nonfat dry milk.*

EGGS means *large eggs.* It is important not to substitute a different size egg. The size of the egg affects the fat content of the recipe and the liquidity (how runny) of the batter.

EGG SUBSTITUTE means *processed egg whites.* Brands, such as EGG BEATERS, are available in food stores.

EGG REPLACER mean the *egg free, lactose free, gluten free Egg Replacer* produced by ENER-G FOODS, INC.

EVAPORATED MILK means a can of *unsweetened evaporated (not condensed) milk.*

GELATIN means *unflavored gelatin.* It is sold under the brand name of KNOX ORIGINAL GELATINE.

LEMON or ORANGE JUICE means *fresh squeezed juice.*

LEMON or ORANGE RIND means *finely grated rind* prepared according to the directions given on page 211.

MARGARINE means sticks of margarine. Not margarine packaged in tubs. Not light margarine. Not whipped margarine.

MARSHMALLOW CREAM is sold under the brand name of JET-PUFFED.

MILK Unless otherwise specified, MILK includes Lactaid milk, low fat, no fat, whole milk and soy milk.

MINUTE TAPIOCA is the brand name for *precooked tapioca*. It is manufactured by KRAFT FOODS GLOBAL, INC.

MOLASSES is sold under the brand name of GRANDMA'S MOLASSES.

SALT means ordinary table salt, not sea salt, not Kosher salt.

SEMI-SWEET BAKING CHOCOLATE is sold under the brand name of BAKER'S SEMI-SWEET BAKING CHOCOLATE SQUARES.

SUGAR means *white granulated sugar.*

VANILLA means *G-F Vanilla Extract.*

WHITE VINEGAR means *distilled white vinegar..* The distilling process removes gluten. Regular vinegar may contain wheat.

YEAST means *dry granulated yeast.*

Cookie Index

Drop Cookies

Don't let the lengthy discussion on the next page discourage you. The drop cookie is easy to bake. Essentially, it's mix, drop on the cookie sheet and bake.

Butter Cookie   18

Mint-Chocolate Cookie   19

Gingersnap   20

Oatmeal Raisin   21

Chocolate Chip   22

Glazed Lemon Drop   23

HOW TO MAKE DROP COOKIES

1. Bring refrigerated ingredients to room temperature (see page 205 explaining how to bring to room temperature).

2. Spray 2 cookie sheets with a G-F unflavored cooking spray. Insulated aluminum or stainless steel cookie sheets are best. They keep the bottom of the cookie from baking too quickly. A Teflon cookie sheet may need a lower baking temperature or less baking time than given in the recipe.

3. Preheat oven to baking temperature given in the **BAKING DIRECTIONS** of the recipe (see page 205, preheating the oven).

4. Sift **DRY INGREDIENTS** into a bowl, then mix with a spoon until blended.

5. Measure **SHORTENING INGREDIENTS** into another bowl. Beat with an electric mixer until blended.

6. Gradually add DRY INGREDIENTS to SHORTENING INGREDIENTS. Stir until blended. If there are **ADDITIONAL INGREDIENTS** such as chocolate chips, raisins, nuts, etc., stir them into the batter.

7. Drop dough by the spoonful onto the cookie sheets. Use a teaspoon for small cookies; a tablespoon for larger cookies. Leave room between for the cookies to spread.

8. Follow **BAKING DIRECTIONS** given in the recipe. Remove cookies from the baking sheet while warm.

BUTTER COOKIE

The Butter Cookie is also known as the Brown Edge Cookie. It is great to eat by itself, or covered with chocolate as in the recipe on the next page.

Follow the DROP COOKIE directions on page 17.

DRY INGREDIENTS

- ☐ 1 1/3 cups G-F CAKE FLOUR
- ☐ 1/2 tsp BAKING POWDER
- ☐ 1/4 tsp SALT
- ☐ 1/2 tsp XANTHAN GUM

SHORTENING INGREDIENTS

- ☐ 1/4 cup BUTTER
- ☐ 1/4 cup BUTTERMILK
- ☐ 2/3 cup SUGAR
- ☐ 1 EGG
- ☐ 1 tsp VANILLA

BAKING DIRECTIONS

Drop by the teaspoon full onto two sprayed cookie sheets. Make 10 cookies per sheet.

Bake at 350° for 20 to 22 minutes till golden brown around the edge.

MINT CHOCOLATE COOKIE

The Mint Chocolate Cookie is a Butter Cookie dipped in a mint chocolate frosting. The cookie has long been a favorite with those who support the annual Girl Scouts fund raiser.

Make Butter Cookies using the recipe on the previous page. Set aside on a wire rack.

MINT CHOCOLATE FROSTING

Heat the following in a double broiler until the CHOCOLATE is melted (see page 204, using a double broiler). Stir till smooth.

- ☐ 4 squares SEMI-SWEET BAKING CHOCOLATE
- ☐ 1/4 cup HEAVY CREAM
- ☐ 2 TBSP BUTTER

Remove from heat and add the following ingredients.

- ☐ 2/3 cup POWDERED SUGAR
- ☐ 3/4 tsp PEPPERMINT EXTRACT

Beat with an electric beater till smooth.

Use kitchen tongs to dip the cookie into the chocolate. Place on a wire rack for an hour until the chocolate sets.

GINGERSNAP

There are different recipes for the popular Gingersnap. This one is based on a Pennsylvania Dutch recipe. It is hard when freshly made, but will soften in a few days. To keep it crisp, store in a tightly sealed cookie tin.

Follow the DROP COOKIE directions on page 17.

DRY INGREDIENTS
- ☐ 1 cup G-F ALL PURPOSE FLOUR
- ☐ 1/2 tsp BAKING SODA
- ☐ 1 1/4 tsp GINGER
- ☐ 1/8 tsp CLOVES
- ☐ 1/2 tsp CINNAMON
- ☐ 1/4 tsp XANTHAN GUM
- ☐ 1/4 tsp CREAM OF TARTAR

SHORTENING INGREDIENTS
- ☐ 1/4 cup BUTTER (or MARGARINE)
- ☐ 1/3 cup SUGAR
- ☐ 1/4 cup MOLASSES

BAKING DIRECTIONS
Drop by the teaspoon onto two sprayed cookie sheets.
Make 12 cookies per sheet.
Sprinkle the top of each cookie with SUGAR.
- ☐ 1 TBSP SUGAR

BAKE at 350° for 15 to 18 minutes or till top is cracked and cookies do not leave an impression when touched.

OATMEAL RAISIN

There are gluten free rolled oats on the market as we went to print, but not the quick cooking oats that are best for baking. The problem is easily solved. Put the rolled oats in a blender and pulse it a few times to make quick cooking oats. 1 3/4 cups of rolled oats will pulse down to the 1 1/2 cups of oats needed for this recipe.

Follow the DROP COOKIE directions on page 17.

DRY INGREDIENTS
- ☐ 1 cup G-F ALL PURPOSE FLOUR
- ☐ 1/2 tsp SALT
- ☐ 3/4 tsp XANTHAN GUM
- ☐ 1/2 tsp BAKING SODA
- ☐ 1/2 tsp ALLSPICE
- ☐ 1 tsp CINNAMON
- ☐ 1/4 tsp CLOVES

SHORTENING INGREDIENTS
- ☐ 1 EGG
- ☐ 1/2 cup BUTTER (or MARGARINE)
- ☐ 1 cup SUGAR

ADDITIONAL INGREDIENTS
- ☐ 1 1/2 cups OATS (quick cooking size)
- ☐ 1/2 cup RAISINS
- ☐ 1/2 cup WALNUTS (coarsely chopped)

BAKING DIRECTIONS
Drop by the tablespoonful onto two cookie sheets.
Make 12 cookies per sheet.

Bake at 375° for 18 to 20 minutes or till slightly brown around the edge.

CHOCOLATE CHIP

There is a wealth of chocolate chips on the market. They vary in size, taste and texture. This is a time to be adventurous. Try different brands of chocolate chips until you find the one that is irresistible.

Follow the DROP COOKIE directions on page 17.

DRY INGREDIENTS
- ☐ 1 1/2 cup G-F ALL PURPOSE FLOUR
- ☐ 1 tsp XANTHAN GUM
- ☐ 1/2 tsp BAKING SODA
- ☐ 1/2 tsp SALT

SHORTENING INGREDIENTS
- ☐ 1/2 cup BUTTER
- ☐ 1 EGG
- ☐ 1/2 cup LIGHT BROWN SUGAR
- ☐ 1/4 cup SUGAR
- ☐ 3/4 tsp VANILLA

ADDITIONAL INGREDIENTS
- ☐ 1 cup SEMI-SWEET CHOCOLATE CHIPS

BAKING DIRECTIONS
Drop by the tablespoon onto two sprayed cookie sheets.
Make 9 cookies per sheet.
Bake at 375° for 15 minutes or till lightly brown around the edge.
Let cookies set on the cookie sheet a few minutes before moving them to a plate.

Food ecstasy is a melt in your mouth, warm from the oven, chocolate chip cookie.

GLAZED LEMON DROP

If your mother enjoyed baking, she probably baked a simple lemon drop cookie — delicious plain, or as in this recipe, with a puckery lemon glaze. Before beginning, take a full, rounded, half cup of cottage cheese and pulse it in a blender until it looks like sour cream. It should blend down to half a cup.

Follow the DROP COOK directions on page 17.

DRY INGREDIENTS
- ☐ 1 cup G-F CAKE FLOUR
- ☐ 1/4 tsp XANTHAN GUM
- ☐ 1/2 tsp BAKING POWDER
- ☐ 1/4 tsp SALT

SHORTENING INGREDIENTS
- ☐ 1/2 cup COTTAGE CHEESE (creamed in blender)
- ☐ 1/4 cup BUTTER
- ☐ 2/3 cup SUGAR
- ☐ 1 EGG
- ☐ 1 tsp LEMON EXTRACT

BAKING DIRECTIONS
Drop by the tablespoon onto two sprayed cookie sheets.
Make 10 cookies per sheet. Bake at 350° for 18 to 20 minutes or till golden brown around the edge.

LEMON GLAZE
Before squeezing the LEMON JUICE make LEMON RIND and LEMON ZEST using 2 or 3 LEMONS (page 211).
Mix the following ingredients together till smooth.
- ☐ 1 cup POWDERED SUGAR
- ☐ 1 tsp LEMON RIND
- ☐ 1 1/2 TBSP LEMON JUICE

Drop 1 tsp of glaze on each cookie. Use a spatula to spread the glaze to the end of the cookie. Before the Glaze hardens, garnish each cookie with one or two strips of Lemon Zest.
- ☐ 1 TBSP LEMON ZEST

Refrigerator Cookies

The thing I miss about refrigerator cookies is the convenience. Buy a tube of cookie dough and bake at home whenever. Now I must first make the batter, but there is a trade-off. These gluten free cookies taste better than their store bought counterpart. See if you don't agree.

Raisin   26

Chocolate Chocolate Chip   27

Chocolate Fudge   28

White Macadamia Nut   29

Snicker Doodle   30

Fruit & Nut   31

HOW TO MAKE REFRIGERATOR COOKIES

The Refrigerator Cookie is the second easiest cookie to bake. It's mix, refrigerate, cut into slices and bake.

1. Bring ingredients to room temperature (page 205).

2. Sift **DRY INGREDIENTS** into a bowl. Mix with a spoon until blended.

3. Measure **SHORTENING INGREDIENTS** into an electric mixing bowl. Beat till creamy.

4. Gradually add DRY INGREDIENTS to the SHORTENING. Mix till blended. If there are **ADDITIONAL INGREDIENTS** such as raisins, nuts, etc., stir them into the batter.

5. Tear off a sheet of parchment baking paper about 12" in length. Turn the dough onto the middle of the paper. Dredge your hands with POWDERED SUGAR and pat dough into a roll 2" in diameter. Increase the diameter for a larger cookie. Starting at the torn edge of the parchment paper, wrap the paper firmly around the dough, three or four times. Tightly twist each end of the paper.

6. The dough needs to be refrigerated for two or more hours in order to set and become firm. The dough can be stored in the refrigerator until you are ready to bake. It is best to use it within 10 days. After that, the dough will begin to dry out.

7. Follow **BAKING DIRECTIONS** given in the recipe. Leave room for the cookies to spread. Remove the cookies from the baking sheet while they are still warm.

RAISIN

The raisin cookie is a simple, but popular, old time favorite. The raisins in this recipe are regular raisins, not the lighter golden raisin, nor the tiny currant — just the usual dark, plump, sweet, California raisin.

Follow the REFRIGERATOR COOKIE directions on page 25.

DRY INGREDIENTS
- ☐   1 1/2 cup G-F CAKE FLOUR
- ☐   1/2 tsp BAKING POWDER
- ☐   1/2 tsp SALT
- ☐   1 tsp XANTHAN GUM

SHORTENING INGREDIENTS
- ☐   7 TBSP BUTTER
- ☐   1 EGG
- ☐   1/3 cup SUGAR
- ☐   1/3 cup BROWN SUGAR
- ☐   1 tsp VANILLA

ADDITIONAL INGREDIENTS
- ☐   2/3 cup RAISINS

For ease of handling divide the dough into two rolls.

BAKING DIRECTIONS

Preheat the oven to 350°. Spray two cookie sheets. Make 10 cookies per cookie sheet.

Bake at 350° for 15 to 20 minutes or till golden brown.

CHOCOLATE CHOCOLATE CHIP

For a chocoholic, the only thing better than a chocolate chip cookie is a chocolate cookie with chocolate chips. Refrigerated dough is easier to cut using mini chocolate chips, however, regular sized chocolate chips work as well. Both sizes were used for the cookies pictured on page 24. The cookie on the left was baked with mini chips. The one on the right with regular sized chocolate chips.

Follow the REFRIGERATOR COOKIE directions on page 25.

DRY INGREDIENTS
- ☐ 1 cup G-F ALL PURPOSE FLOUR
- ☐ 2 TBSP BAKING COCOA
- ☐ 1/2 tsp XANTHAN GUM
- ☐ 1/2 tsp BAKING SODA
- ☐ 1/4 tsp SALT

SHORTENING INGREDIENTS
- ☐ 1/3 cup BUTTER
- ☐ 1 EGG
- ☐ 1/3 cup LIGHT BROWN SUGAR
- ☐ 1/4 cup SUGAR
- ☐ 1/2 tsp VANILLA

ADDITIONAL INGREDIENTS
- ☐ 3/4 cup SEMI-SWEET CHOCOLATE CHIPS

BAKING DIRECTIONS

Preheat the oven to 350°. Spray two cookie sheets.
Cut the dough into 1/2" slices. Make 8 cookies per cookie sheet.

Bake at 350° for 22 minutes or till golden brown.

CHOCOLATE FUDGE

This is a thick, fudgy, chocolate cookie — sure to satisfy a craving for chocolate. The cookie is made with melted chocolate chips. Different chips have different sugar and cocoa content. If you find the cookie too sweet or not sweet enough, try a different chip before changing the amount of sugar in the recipe.

Sift and mix DRY INGREDIENTS.

DRY INGREDIENTS
- ☐ 2/3 cup G-F ALL PURPOSE FLOUR
- ☐ 1/8 tsp salt   ☐ 1/2 tsp BAKING POWDER

Beat EGG with a hand held electric mixer for 3 minutes, then gradually beat in SUGAR.

EGG MIXTURE
- ☐ 1 EGG   ☐ 1/2 cup SUGAR

Melt CHOCOLATE MIXTURE in a microwave oven, stirring every 20 seconds till blended.

CHOCOLATE MIXTURE
- ☐ 1 cup SEMI-SWEET CHOCOLATE CHIPS
- ☐ 3 TBSP BUTTER (or MARGARINE)

Stir CHOCOLATE MIXTURE into EGG MIXTURE, then gradually add the DRY INGREDIENTS.

Form and refrigerate the dough following steps 5 and 6 of the directions given on page 25.

BAKING DIRECTIONS
Preheat oven to 350°. Spray 2 cookie sheets.
Cut dough into 1/2" slices making 8 cookies per sheet.
Bake at 350° for 15 to 18 minutes.

WHITE MACADAMIA NUT

This crispy, white chocolate, macadamia nut cookie became a refrigerator cookie favorite over the past several years. If you did not enjoy it prior to eating G-F, you're in for a treat.

Follow the REFRIGERATOR COOKIE directions on page 25.

DRY INGREDIENTS
- ☐ 1 1/2 cup G-F ALL PURPOSE FLOUR
- ☐ 1/2 tsp BAKING SODA
- ☐ 1/2 tsp SALT
- ☐ 3/4 tsp XANTHAN GUM

SHORTENING INGREDIENTS
- ☐ 1/2 cup BUTTER
- ☐ 1 EGG
- ☐ 2/3 cup SUGAR
- ☐ 1/2 cup LIGHT BROWN SUGAR
- ☐ 1 tsp VANILLA

ADDITIONAL INGREDIENTS
- ☐ 1/2 cup WHITE CHOCOLATE CHIPS
- ☐ 1/2 cup MACADAMIA NUTS (chopped)

For ease of handling divide the dough into two rolls.
Each roll makes 8 to 10 cookies depending on the diameter of the roll of dough.

BAKING DIRECTIONS
Preheat the oven to 350°. Spray two large cookie sheets.
Cut the dough into 1/2" slices. Divide the cookies evenly between the two cookie sheets. Leave room to spread.

Bake at 350° for 20 minutes or till golden brown.

SNICKER DOODLE

There is no one recipe for the Snicker Doodle. The Pennsylvania Dutch make it with raisins and nuts. New England recipes call for a buttery cookie with spiced topping — sometimes nutmeg, sometimes cinnamon. We choose a Snicker Doodle recipe with a cinnamon pecan topping for no particular reason other than it tastes good.

Follow the REFRIGERATOR COOKIE directions on page 25.

DRY INGREDIENTS

☐ 1 cup G-F CAKE FLOUR
☐ 1/2 tsp XANTHAN GUM   ☐ 1/4 tsp SALT

SHORTENING INGREDIENTS

☐ 1 EGG   ☐ 6 TBSP BUTTER
☐ 6 TBSP SUGAR   ☐ 1/2 TBSP VANILLA

BAKING DIRECTIONS

Preheat oven to 350°.
Blend the CINNAMON MIXTURE in a small bowl.

CINNAMON MIXTURE

☐ 1/4 tsp CINNAMON   ☐ 2 TBSP SUGAR

Cut PECAN HALVES lengthwise making PECAN QUARTERS.

☐ 30 PECAN QUARTERS

BAKING DIRECTIONS

Preheat oven to 350°. Spray 3 cookie sheets. Slice dough into thin slices, each a little less than a quarter of an inch. Make 10 cookies per baking sheet leaving room to spread.
Brush each cookie with EGG WHITE

☐ **1 EGG WHITE** (slightly beaten)

Sprinkle with CINNAMON MIXTURE, then place a PECAN QUARTER in the center of each cookie. Bake at 350° for 12-15 minutes or till golden brown around the edge.

FRUIT & NUT

A better name for this cookie might be the Designer Cookie because the choice of fruit and nut is yours. You can use any kind of chopped dried fruit or use a fruit mix such as Sun Maid Fruit Bits or Sun Maid Tropical Trio. Walnuts go well with dried fruit. Pecans, cashews, macadamia nuts, almonds or a chopped nut mixture, can also be used. It's up to you. Each cookie baked will be an expression of your own unique taste.

Follow the REFRIGERATOR COOKIE directions on page 25.

DRY INGREDIENTS

☐ 1 1/2 cup G-F CAKE FLOUR   ☐ 1/2 tsp SALT
☐ 1/2 tsp BAKING SODA   ☐ 1 tsp XANTHAN GUM

SHORTENING INGREDIENTS

☐ 7 TBSP BUTTER   ☐ 1 EGG
☐ 2/3 cup SUGAR   ☐ 1 tsp VANILLA

ADDITIONAL INGREDIENTS

☐ 1 cup DRIED FRUIT PIECES   ☐ 1 cup chopped NUTS

For ease of handling divide the dough into two rolls.
Each roll makes 10 cookies.

BAKING DIRECTIONS

Preheat the oven to 350°. Spray two cookie sheets.
Cut dough into 1/2" slices.
Make 10 cookies per sheet leaving room to spread.

Bake at 350° for 20 minutes or till golden brown.

Bar Cookies

*Chocolate-Nut Biscotti 35
and Almond Biscotti 34*

Breakfast Bar 36

"Graham" Crackers 38

Chocolate "Grahams" 39

S'More 40

Shortbread Cookie 41

Lemon Bar 42

Brownie 43

HOW TO MAKE BAR COOKIES

The Bar Cookie is another easy to make cookie. The ingredients are mixed much the same as the Drop Cookie. The dough is spread or poured into a baking pan and then baked. It is cut into bars after baking.

1. Unless recipe indicates otherwise, bring ingredients to room temperature (page 205).

2. Spray the baking pan and preheat the oven as directed at the beginning of the recipe.

3. Sift **DRY INGREDIENTS** into a bowl, then mix with a spoon.

4. Measure **SHORTENING INGREDIENTS** into an electric mixer and beat till blended.

5. Add **EGGS** to SHORTENING INGREDIENTS beating well after each addition.

6. Stir DRY INGREDIENTS into SHORTENING mixture until blended.

7. Fold in **FRUIT** or **NUTS**, if any.

8. Follow **BAKING DIRECTIONS** given in the recipe to form and bake the cookies.

ALMOND BISCOTTI

The Italian word *Biscotto* means "twice baked." The biscuit is baked as a loaf and then cut and baked again till toasty. This popular treat is available in coffee shops in many flavors with Almond and Chocolate-Nut the most popular.

Preheat oven to 350°. Spray a cookie sheet.
Follow BAR COOKIE directions on page 33.

DRY INGREDIENTS
☐ 1 cup + 1 TBSP G-F CAKE FLOUR
☐ 1 tsp XANTHAN GUM
☐ 1 tsp BAKING POWDER   ☐ 1/8 tsp SALT

SHORTENING INGREDIENTS
☐ 2 TBSP CRISCO   ☐ 1/2 cup SUGAR
☐ 3/4 tsp ALMOND EXTRACT

EGG   ☐ 1 EGG

NUTS   ☐ 1/4 cup ALMONDS (coarsely chopped)
Work the nuts into the batter with your hands.

BAKING DIRECTIONS
Place the dough in the middle of a sprayed cookie sheet.
Pat it into a loaf 8" long and 3" wide.
Bake at 350° for 20 to 22 minutes until golden brown.
Cool to room temperature (not warm) on the cookie sheet.
Use a thin, sharp, knife to cut the loaf into 9 biscuits.

Second Baking
Preheat oven to 400°. Place the biscuits cut side up on a sprayed cookie sheet. Bake at 400° for 12 to 15 minutes till toasty brown. Cool to room temperature before removing from the cookie sheet.

CHOCOLATE-NUT BISCOTTI

The Chocolate-Nut Biscotti pictured on page 32 was baked with pecan pieces, but any nut will do. Try an unsalted or lightly salted cocktail nut mix for a gourmet Biscotti.

Preheat oven to 350°. Spray a cookie sheet.
Follow BAR COOKIE DIRECTIONS on page 33.

DRY INGREDIENTS
- ☐ 1 cup G-F ALL PURPOSE FLOUR
- ☐ 1 tsp BAKING POWDER ☐ 1/8 tsp SALT
- ☐ 2 TBSP BAKING COCOA ☐ 1 tsp XANTHAN GUM
- ☐ 1 tsp COFFEE GRANULES

SHORTENING INGREDIENTS
- ☐ 2 TBSP CRISCO
- ☐ 3/4 cup SUGAR
- ☐ 1/2 tsp VANILLA

EGG ☐ 1 EGG

NUTS ☐ 1/4 cup NUTS (coarsely chopped)
Work the nuts into the batter with your hands.

BAKING DIRECTIONS
Place the dough in the middle of a sprayed cookie sheet.
Pat it into a loaf 8" long and 4" wide.
Bake at 350° for 22 to 25 minutes until brown around the edges.
Cool to room temperature (not warm) on the cookie sheet.
Use a thin, sharp, knife to cut the loaf into 9 biscuits.

Second Baking
Preheat oven to 400°. Place the biscuits cut side up on sprayed cookie sheet. Bake at 400° for 10 minutes. Cool to room temperature before removing from the cookie sheet.

BREAKFAST BAR

The Breakfast Bar is not just for breakfast. It can be a nutritious snack for an afternoon pick me up, or a healthful treat to take along for a picnic or outing. The Basic Breakfast Bar Recipe can be used with your choice of fruits and nuts or use either of the FRUIT AND NUT COMBINATIONS given on the next page.

BASIC BREAKFAST BAR RECIPE

Preheat oven to 325°. Spray a rectangular pan (9" X 13"). Follow the BAR COOKIE directions on page 33.

DRY INGREDIENTS
- ☐ 1 1/2 cups G-F ALL PURPOSE FLOUR
- ☐ 1 tsp XANTHAN GUM
- ☐ 1 1/2 tsp BAKING POWDER
- ☐ 1/4 tsp SALT

SHORTENING INGREDIENTS
- ☐ 1/2 cup APPLE SAUCE
- ☐ 1/2 cup BUTTER
- ☐ 1/2 cup HONEY
- ☐ 1/2 cup BROWN SUGAR

EGGS
- ☐ 2 EGGS

Fold in the OAT MIXTURE.

OAT MIXTURE
- ☐ 1 cup SWEETENED COCONUT FLAKES
- ☐ 1 cup OATS (Use a blender to make Rolled Oats quick cooking size. See top of page 21.)

Fold in 2 cups of DRIED FRUIT and 2 cups of CHOPPED NUTS. Use any blend of your favorite dried fruit and nuts or try the **TRADITIONAL BAR MIXTURE** or the **TROPICAL BAR MIXTURE** on the next page.

BREAKFAST BAR

FRUIT AND NUT COMBINATIONS

TRADITIONAL BAR MIXTURE

These ingredients are traditionally included in BREAKFAST BARS.

- ☐ 1 cup RAISINS
- ☐ 1 cup DRIED CRANBERRIES
- ☐ 1 cup SUNFLOWER SEEDS
- ☐ 1 cup PUMPKIN SEEDS

TROPICAL BAR MIXTURE

These ingredients give a sweeter, more tropical flavor to the BREAKFAST BAR.

- ☐ 1 cup SUN MAID TROPICAL TRIO
  (dried Pineapple, Papaya, Mango)
- ☐ 1 cup DRIED DATE PIECES
- ☐ 1 cup SLIVERED ALMONDS
- ☐ 1 cup WALNUTS PIECES

BAKING DIRECTIONS

Spread the batter evenly into a sprayed rectangular pan.
Bake at 325° for 30 minutes or till golden brown around the edge.
While in the pan cut into 4 sections vertically and 4 sections horizontally, making 16 Breakfast Bars.

"GRAHAM" CRACKERS

Graham crackers are made from wheat bran. I substituted rice bran and got a RFT (Reasonable Facsimile Thereof). Making the cracker look like a graham cracker takes a bit a work, but it's worth the effort to once again enjoy a Chocolate Covered Graham and a S'more (pages 39 & 40).

Preheat the oven to 325°.
Liberally spray 2 glass square baking pans (8" X 8" X 2").
Sift and mix DRY INGREDIENTS.

DRY INGREDIENTS

☐	1 cup G-F ALL PURPOSE FLOUR	☐ 1/4 cup RICE BRAN
☐	3 TBSP ALMOND MEAL	☐ 1/4 cup SUGAR
☐	1/2 tsp BAKING POWDER	☐ 1/2 tsp CINNAMON
☐	3/4 tsp XANTHAN GUM	☐ 1/4 tsp SALT

Cut the BUTTER into the DRY INGREDIENTS (page 208).
      ☐ 1/4 cup BUTTER (cold from refrigerator)
Add LIQUID INGREDIENTS.

LIQUID INGREDIENTS

    ☐ 1 TBSP HONEY   ☐ 1 TBSP LIGHT CORN SYRUP
    ☐ 1/2 tsp VANILLA

Work dough with your hands until it forms a ball. Crumble half of the dough into each sprayed square pan. Use the back of a measuring cup to press the dough into a smooth thin layer that covers the bottom, not the sides. Straighten the edges with a butter knife. Use a small sharp knife to cut the dough into thirds horizontally and vertically making 9 crackers per pan. Use a fork to prick 4 straight lines into each cracker.

OPTIONAL CINNAMON TOPPING

Stir SUGAR and CINNAMON with a spoon till blended.
    ☐ 1/4 cup SUGAR   ☐ 1/2 tsp CINNAMON
Before baking, sprinkle the sugar mixture evenly over the crackers.

"GRAHAM" CRACKERS

BAKING DIRECTIONS

Bake at 325 for 10 minutes. Remove from the oven.
Cut through the straight lines reforming the 9 squares.
Bake for another 12 to 15 minutes till edges are lightly brown.

Let the crackers cool to room temperature in the baking pan. Loosen the crackers by cutting through the straight lines and the outer edge with a sharp knife. Once cut, the crackers should pop out with no breaking or crumbling.

CHOCOLATE "GRAHAMS"

Make 18 "Graham" Crackers without the Cinnamon Topping.

GLOSSY CHOCOLATE FROSTING

Melt BUTTER in the micro in a mixing bowl.

☐ 3 TBSP BUTTER

Stir in the following in the order given:

☐ 1/ 3 cup BAKING COCOA
☐ 1 tsp LIGHT CORN SYRUP
☐ 1 tsp VANILLA

Alternate POWDERED SUGAR and MILK until spreading consistency. Begin and end with POWDERED SUGAR. Stir well after each addition.

☐ 2 cups POWDERED SUGAR   ☐ 1/ 4 cup MILK

Before frosting, use a pastry brush to remove loose crumbs from the cracker. You can dip the cracker into the frosting with kitchen tongs. Problem is (brushing notwithstanding) crumbs will fall into the frosting. By the 18th cracker the frosting will "crummy." To avoid the problem hold the cracker on its edge and use a butter knife to frost the cracker. Place the frosted cracker on a wire rack. Let it set for an hour for the frosting to harden.

S'MORES

You can make S'mores by putting marshmallows and chocolate between "Graham" crackers and heating until the marshmallows and chocolate melt. It will taste good. Making your own marshmallow and melted chocolate filling tastes a whole lot better.

Make two square pans of crackers without the optional topping. When room temperature, remove the crackers from one pan. Loosen the crackers from the other pan, but leave them in place.

MARSHMALLOW

Put WATER in a saucepan and sprinkle it with GELATIN.

☐ 1 package (2 1/2 tsp) GELATIN   ☐ 1/3 cup COLD WATER

Let stand for 5 minutes till softened, then cook over low heat until dissolved. Add SUGAR and bring to a boil.

☐ 1/3 cup SUGAR

Pour GELATIN mixture into a electric mixer bowl with whisk attachment. Beat on high while slowly dribbling in CORN SYRUP, then VANILLA.

☐ 1/3 cup LIGHT CORN SYRUP   ☐ 1/2 tsp VANILLA

Beat on high for 20 minutes until MARSHMALLOW consistency. Pour the MARSHMALLOW over the baked crackers in the pan. Let stand for a half hour to set.

CHOCOLATE FILLING

Stir the following ingredients in a double broiler until the CHOCOLATE is melted (page 204).

☐ 4 squares SEMI-SWEET BAKING CHOCOLATE
☐ 1/4 cup HEAVY CREAM   ☐ 2 TBSP BUTTER

Remove from heat and beat in POWDERED SUGAR with an electric beater till spreading consistency.

☐ 1 cup POWDERED SUGAR

Spread the CHOCOLATE FILLING over the MARSHMALLOW layer. Cover the chocolate with the remaining "Graham" Cracker squares. Remove the S'mores from the pan and enjoy.

SHORTBREAD COOKIE

The shortbread cookie is a rich, buttery cookie that originated in Scotland. Like many overseas treats, the cookie became popular in the US. It is sold in bakeries as well as the packaged cookie section of the supermarket. This recipe comes close in taste and texture to Lorna Doone, the popular shortbread cookie made by Nabisco.

Preheat oven to 350º.
Spray a square baking pan (8" X 8" X 2").

Follow BAR COOKIE directions on page 33.

DRY INGREDIENTS
- ☐ 1 cup G-F ALL PURPOSE FLOUR
- ☐ 1/2 tsp XANTHAN GUM
- ☐ 1/2 tsp BAKING POWDER
- ☐ 1/4 tsp SALT

SHORTENING INGREDIENTS
- ☐ 1/4 cup BUTTER FLAVORED CRISCO
- ☐ 1/2 cup POWDERED SUGAR

EGGS
- ☐ 2 EGG YOLKS

Spread dough evenly in a square pan. Use the back of a spoon to press the dough together. Use a spatula to smooth the edges of the dough. Use a fork to make an indentation design and to even the dough (see picture page 32). Cut the dough into quarters vertically and into quarters horizontally, making 16 squares.

BAKING DIRECTIONS
Bake at 350º until slightly brown around the edges (12 to 15 minutes). Remove from oven. Loosen the cookies by recutting the lines with a sharp knife. Place the 16 squares onto a sprayed cookie sheet. Bake another 10 minutes or till golden brown.

LEMON BAR

The Lemon Bar has a pastry bottom made much like a pie crust. The filling is poured over the baked crust and returned to the oven to finish baking. This is a good company dessert because it can be made the day before, and topped with powdered sugar just before serving.

Preheat oven to 350°. Spray a square pan (8" X 8" X 2").

PASTRY LAYER
Sift and mix DRY INGREDIENTS.

DRY INGREDIENTS
- ☐ 1 cup G-F ALL PURPOSE FLOUR   ☐ 1/3 cup SUGAR
- ☐ 3/4 tsp XANTHAN GUM   ☐ 1/8 tsp SALT

Cut BUTTER into DRY INGREDIENTS (page 208).
- ☐ 1/3 cup BUTTER (cold from refrigerator)

Use your hands to mix dough into a ball. Spread dough into a sprayed square pan. Use the bottom of a measuring cup to press the dough into a smooth layer.

BAKING DIRECTIONS
Bake 350° for 20 minutes or till slightly brown around the edge. Meanwhile make FILLING INGREDIENTS.

FILLING INGREDIENTS
- ☐ 1 tsp LEMON RIND (page 211)   ☐ 4 EGGS
- ☐ 1/3 cup LEMON JUICE   ☐ 1 cup SUGAR
- ☐ 3 TBSP G-F ALL PURPOSE FLOUR   ☐ 1/8 tsp SALT

Beat FILLING INGREDIENTS on low speed till blended.
Gently pour the FILLING onto the hot baked crust.

BAKING DIRECTIONS
Lower heat to 325° and bake for 20 minutes until the center is set; i.e., doesn't jiggle when moved. Let cool in pan, then cut into 9 squares. Refrigerate till ready to serve, then sprinkle with POWDERED SUGAR.   ☐ **2 TBSP POWDERED SUGAR**

BROWNIE

The Brownie is the most popular bar cookie. There are all kinds of Brownie recipes, from chocolate cake type Brownies to chocolate frosted Brownies, and even "blonde" Brownies with no chocolate at all. The traditional Brownie is rich and fudgy and that is the recipe given below.

Spray a square pan (8" X 8" x 2"). Preheat oven to 375°.
Sift and mix DRY INGREDIENTS.

DRY INGREDIENTS
- [ ] 1/2 cup G-F ALL PURPOSE FLOUR
- [ ] 1/2 tsp BAKING POWDER
- [ ] 1/4 tsp XANTHAN GUM   [ ] 1/4 tsp SALT

SHORTENING INGREDIENTS
Use the paddle attachment to an electric mixer to beat BUTTER and SUGAR until creamy.
- [ ] 1/4 cup BUTTER   [ ] 1/2 cup SUGAR

Add EGGS, one at a time, and then VANILLA, beating well after each addition.
- [ ] 2 EGGS   [ ] 1/2 tsp VANILLA

Melt CHOCOLATE CHIPS in a microwave oven stirring every 30 seconds till melted.
- [ ] 1 cup SEMI-SWEET CHOCOLATE CHIPS

Beat melted chocolate into shortening mixture.
Stir DRY INGREDIENTS into shortening mixture till blended.
Fold in WALNUTS   [ ] 1/2 cup WALNUTS (chopped)

BAKING DIRECTIONS
Pour batter into sprayed square baking pan. Top with WALNUTS.
- [ ] 1/3 cup WALNUT PIECES

Bake at 350° for 25 to 30 minutes till slightly brown around edge. Cool to room temperature in baking pan, then cut into 9 squares.

Shaped Cookies

This section has two types of shaped cookies starting with the easiest to make — the hand shaped cookie (Peanut Butter, Sesame Seed, etc.). The second type of shaped cookie is the cut-out cookie (Sugar and Gingerbread).

Peanut Butter Cookie   45

Sesame Seed Cookie   46

Pignoli Cookie   47

Pfeffernusse   48

Cut-out Sugar Cookie   52

Gingerbread Man & Cut-outs 53

PEANUT BUTTER COOKIE

The Peanut Butter Cookie pictured on the opposite page was made with extra chunky peanut butter, but you can make this cookie with any peanut butter: smooth, chunky, low fat. This is an easy recipe to make, so experiment with different peanut butters until you find the taste and texture you like best.

Spray two cookie sheets. Preheat oven to 350°

Put all of the ingredients into a blender or food processor with blade attachment. Pulse into a smooth ball.

- [ ] 1 cup PEANUT BUTTER
- [ ] 1 1/2 TBSP G-F ALL PURPOSE FLOUR
- [ ] 1 EGG
- [ ] 2/3 cup SUGAR
- [ ] 1/2 tsp VANILLA

Refrigerate the dough for an hour.

Form 1" balls. Make 8 cookies per sheet. Leave room to spread. Make decorative squares by pressing a fork into the dough and making horizontal lines and then vertical lines.

BAKING DIRECTIONS
Bake at 350° for 25 to 30 minutes till slightly brown around the edge. Let cool for a minute before removing the cookies from the baking sheet.

SESAME SEED BISCUIT

This Sesame Seed Biscuit is called Biscotta di Regina (the Queen's Biscuits). More snack than dessert, it is a mid-morning pick me up to accompany a favorite beverage, or a royal cure for a case of the munchies.

Put CRISCO in the freezer for an hour prior to mixing.
Heat oven to 375°. Spray two cookie sheets.

Sift and mix the DRY INGREDIENTS.
DRY INGREDIENTS
- ☐ 2 cups G-F ALL PURPOSE FLOUR
- ☐ 1 1/2 TBSP BAKING POWDER   ☐ 1/2 cup SUGAR
- ☐ 1 1/2 tsp XANTHAN GUM   ☐ 1/8 tsp SALT

Cut SHORTENING into DRY INGREDIENTS (page 208).
- ☐ 6 TBSP CRISCO
- ☐ 2 TBSP COLD BUTTER

Add LIQUID INGREDIENTS.
LIQUID INGREDIENTS
- ☐ 1 EGG (slightly beaten)
- ☐ 1/4 cup COLD MILK

Use your hands to make a soft dough.
Form 18 one inch balls.
Mold each into a football shape (see picture on page 44).

Measure SESAME SEEDS into a small bowl.
- ☐ 3/4 cup SESAME SEEDS

Roll each biscuit liberally in SESAME SEEDS.
Place 9 biscuits on each sprayed cookie sheet.

BAKING DIRECTIONS
Bake at 375° for 15 minutes or till golden brown.

PIGNOLI (PINE NUT COOKIE)

This is another Italian favorite (Did you guess I am Italian?). This cookie is made with almond paste. I could not find a commercial almond paste that did not contain wheat, so I substituted ground almonds — with excellent results.

Put the following ingredients in a saucepan and beat with a hand held electric mixer till it blends into a ball.

- ☐ 1 1/2 cups ALMOND MEAL (packed)
- ☐ 1/8 TSP SALT
- ☐ 2 EGG WHITES
- ☐ 1 cup SUGAR

Cook over low heat stirring with a wooden spoon for 5 minutes until dough is warm.

Remove form heat. Add ALMOND EXTRACT and beat with an electric mixer for 2 minutes till smooth.

- ☐ 1 tsp ALMOND EXTRACT

Put in refrigerator for several hours or overnight.

Preheat oven to 350°. Spray two cookie sheets.
Roll the dough into 14 balls.
Set up three bowls:

1st bowl	☐	1/3 cup POWDERED SUGAR
2nd bowl	☐	1 EGG WHITE (beaten till foamy)
3rd bowl	☐	1 cup PIGNOLIS (pine nuts)

Roll each ball into the bowl ingredients in the given order.
Press the PIGNOLIS into the dough so they will not drop off while baking. Place 7 cookies on each baking sheet.

BAKING DIRECTIONS

Bake at 350° for 10 minutes. Reduce heat to 325° and continue to bake another 12 minutes or till golden brown.
When room temperature sprinkle with POWDERED SUGAR and serve.

PFEFFERNUSSE

Pfeffernusse is the German word for "pepper nut." It is also the name of a spicy cookie that contains ground pepper. The cookie is covered with a hard white frosting. It is stored in an air-tight container for two weeks after baking to allow the spices to blend. It is a great cookie for the holidays because it is baked way before the holiday crunch.

SUBSTITUTIONS

A quarter teaspoon of Cardamon and a quarter teaspoon of Mace are spices traditionally included this recipe. Problem is Cardamon and Mace are expensive and rarely used in other recipes. Unless you bake Pfeffernusse for a living, these spices will sit in your pantry till they (or you) die of old age. For a RFT (Reasonable Facsimile Thereof), we omitted the Cardamon and substituted Nutmeg for Mace.

Follow the directions for Refrigerator Cookies on page 25.

DRY INGREDIENTS

- [ ] 1 1/2 cups G-F ALL PURPOSE FLOUR
- [ ] 1/4 tsp BAKING POWDER   - [ ] 1/4 tsp BAKING SODA
- [ ] 3/4 tsp XANTHAN GUM
- [ ] 1/4 tsp ALLSPICE   - [ ] 1/4 tsp NUTMEG
- [ ] 1/8 tsp ANISE SEED EXTRACT   - [ ] 1/8 tsp SALT
- [ ] 1/4 tsp GROUND WHITE PEPPER

SHORTENING MIXTURE

- [ ] 1/3 cup HONEY   - [ ] 1 1/2 TBSP BUTTER
- [ ] 1 EGG YOLK   - [ ] 2 TBSP SUGAR

PFEFFERNUSSE

BAKING DIRECTIONS

Heat oven to 350°. Spray one cookie sheet. Divide dough into 12 one inch balls. Bake 15 minutes until the top is cracked and bottom slightly brown.

PFEFFERNUSSE FROSTING

Add DRIED EGG WHITES to WARM WATER and stir for 2 minutes until the powder is absorbed into the water.

☐ 1 TBSP DRIED EGG WHITES (JUST WHITES)
☐ 2 TBSP WARM WATER

Beat with a hand held electric mixer till peaks form.
Beat the HONEY into the beaten egg whites.

☐ 1 tsp HONEY

Gradually add POWDERED SUGAR until the frosting is of dipping consistency.

☐ up to 1 1/2 cups POWDERED SUGAR

Dip cookies in icing and put on wire rack to dry.

DOUBLE DIPPING

For a thicker frosting, let the first coat of frosting harden for a couple of hours, then mix another batch of frosting. Dip the cookies a second time and let them harden once again.

RIPENING THE COOKIE

Store the cookies in an air-tight container for 2 or more weeks before serving to allow the spices flavors to blend into each other.

HOW TO MAKE CUT-OUT COOKIES

MIXING THE DOUGH

1. Bring refrigerated items to room temperature
2. Sift and mix the DRY INGREDIENTS
3. Cream the SHORTENING INGREDIENTS.
4. Add the DRY INGREDIENTS to the SHORTENING.
   Work with your hand into a smooth ball.

DOUGH TEXTURE

The dough needs to be dry enough not to stick to your hands, but not so dry that it crumbles. If the dough is crumbly, add a teaspoon of water. If it is "sticky" place it in the refrigerator until firm enough to roll (usually 30 minutes).

ROLLING THE DOUGH

Handle the dough lightly and as little as possible. It's easier to work with a small amount of dough, so divide the dough into two parts. Roll out the dough between a silicone mat and a sheet of wax paper, or two sheets of waxed paper. Dust the silicone mat and the top of the dough with RICE FLOUR. Roll the dough 1/4" thick or to your desired thickness. Thick dough will bake into a cake like cookie. Thin dough makes a crisper cookie.

FORMING THE COOKIE

A star shaped cookie cutter kit was used to make the Christmas Tree pictured on page 44. Peppermint candy separates the layers of cookies. A cookie Christmas Tree can be made without a kit by making a series of round cookies, each one smaller than the last. The base layer will be too large to move from the silicon mat to the cookie sheet, so roll the dough directly on a side-less cookie sheet. Remove the excess dough with the cookie cutter in place on the side-less cookie sheet. Large Gingerbread Man cookies are also best rolled on a side-less cookie sheet. That's better than risking bent back or lost limb in the move from silicone mat to cookie sheet.

DECORATING THE CUT-OUT COOKIE

DECORATING BEFORE BAKING

You can sprinkle decorative sugars onto the cookie before baking. To make the sugar stick to the dough, brush the surface of the cookie with EGG SUBSTITUTE.

DECORATING AFTER BAKING

Once the cookie is baked, decorate with the DECORATIVE GLAZE (page 52) or with DECORATIVE ICING sold in tubes. They come in a variety of colors, white, red, pink, purple, yellow, etc.

DECORATIVE ICING

Decorative icing is easily made with POWDERED SUGAR and WATER. Measure the sugar into a small bowl. Add water a teaspoon at a time. Stir well after each addition. The icing should be thick, yet of spreading consistency.

- ☐ 1 cup POWDERED SUGAR
- ☐ up to 4 tsp WATER

COLORING THE ICING

Separate the icing into two small bowls to color. You can leave the icing in the first bowl white and put a drop or two of food coloring in the second bowl or color the icing in both bowls. The three primary food colors: red, yellow, blue, can be used to make any other color (yellow and blue make green, red and blue make purple, etc.).

DECORATING THE COOKIE

Once the icing is made pour it into a plastic bag with a top that seals. Seal the top, then cut a small hole in one of the bottom corners. Decorate the cookie by gently squeezing the top of the plastic bag.

CUT-OUT SUGAR COOKIE

Making Cut-Out Sugar Cookies is the most fun when made with children helpers. They can use cookie cutters to make their favorite shapes and their imagination to decorate the baked cookie.

Spray 2 cookie sheets. Preheat oven to 350⁰.
Follow the CUT-OUT COOKIE directions on page 50.

DRY INGREDIENTS
- ☐ 1 1/2 cup G-F ALL PURPOSE FLOUR
- ☐ 1 1/2 tsp XANTHAN GUM
- ☐ 1/4 tsp SALT

SHORTENING INGREDIENTS
- ☐ 1/3 cup BUTTER
- ☐ 1/4 cup EGG SUBSTITUTE
- ☐ 1/2 cup SUGAR
- ☐ 1 tsp VANILLA

BAKING DIRECTIONS
Bake at 350⁰ for 15 to 20 minutes or till slightly brown around the edges.

Decorate the cookies using the directions on page 51 or cover with a DECORATIVE GLAZE (see heart shaped cookie page 44).

DECORATIVE GLAZE
Mix till smooth. Use a butter knife to spread on cookie.
- ☐ 1 cup POWDERED SUGAR
- ☐ 2 TBSP MILK
- ☐ few drops FOOD COLORING

GINGERBREAD MAN

The most popular shape for a Gingerbread Cookie is the Gingerbread man. You can use raisins to give him eyes and a big smile before baking or use Decorative Icing (page 51) to glue on the raisins after baking.

Spray 2 cookie sheets. Preheat oven to 350°.
Follow the CUT-OUT COOKIE directions on page 50.

DRY INGREDIENTS

☐ 1 1/3 cup G-F ALL PURPOSE FLOUR
☐ 1 1/4 tsp XANTHAN GUM
☐ 1/4 tsp SALT
☐ 1 tsp BAKING POWDER
☐ 1 tsp GINGER
☐ 1/2 tsp CINNAMON
☐ 1/8 tsp CLOVES

SHORTENING INGREDIENTS

☐ 1/4 cup BUTTER or MARGARINE
☐ 6 TBSP SUGAR
☐ 1/4 cup MOLASSES

BAKING DIRECTIONS

Bake at 350° for 15 minutes or till slightly golden around the edges.

Once baked, loosen the cookie from the baking sheet with a spatula. Let them cool to room temperature on the cookie sheet.

Cake Index

Cake Index

The Basic Cake

White Cake   60

Yellow Cake   62

Sponge - Strawberry 64

Sponge - Banana 64

Chocolate Cake 66

Angel Food Cake 68

Raisin Spice Cake 70

Pound Cake   72

CAKE BAKING TIPS

Baking a cake is no more difficult than baking a drop cookie. You mix the ingredients, pour into a pan and bake. However, a cake is more "temperamental." It is sensitive to the way it is mixed, changes in temperature and air pressure (sea level or mountain top). Even banging the oven door shut while baking can make a cake sink.

To get the best results:

☑ Have all ingredients at room temperature.

☑ Use exact measures. A teaspoon is a level teaspoon, not a rounded teaspoon.

☑ "Cream shortening and sugar till light and fluffy" means to beat the shortening till smooth. Gradually add the sugar while continuing to beat.

☑ "Alternate dry and liquid ingredients" means to:

— gradually stir a third of the dry ingredients into the creamed mixture with a spatula or large spoon

— stir in half the liquid ingredients.

— stir in half of the remaining dry ingredients.

— stir in the rest of the liquid ingredients.

— stir in the rest of the dry ingredients.

   Stir till blended after each addition.

☑ Pour batter into cake pan. Cake will rise in the middle, so spread batter towards the edges leaving the middle slightly indented.

☑ Check your oven temperature with a separate oven thermometer. Some ovens increase in temperature while baking, so check the temperature at the beginning of the bake cycle, and then at 20 minute intervals.

☑ Leave the oven light on to see when cake begins to pull away from the sides. The cake is done when you can press the cake in the middle without leaving an impression. To double check, insert a toothpick in the middle of the cake. If it comes out clean (without batter sticking to it), the cake is done.

HOW TO BAKE A CAKE

1. Bring refrigerated items (eggs, milk, butter) to room temperature (page 205).

2. Prepare the cake pan(s) using the directions given in the recipe. For a tall cake with more filling and frosting than cake in each bite use three 8" cake pans. Use two 9" cake pans to accent the taste of the cake over the frosting and filling.

3. Preheat oven to the temperature given in the **BAKING DIRECTIONS**.

4. Sift **DRY INGREDIENTS** into a bowl. Mix with a large spoon.

5. Measure **LIQUID INGREDIENTS** into another bowl.

6. Measure **SHORTENING INGREDIENTS** into electric mixing bowl. Beat till light and fluffy (3 minutes).

7. Add **EGGS** to **SHORTENING** INGREDIENTS one at a time, beating well after each addition.

8. Alternate **DRY** and **LIQUID INGREDIENTS** into **SHORTENING** (see directions on last page).

9. Pour batter into baking pan(s).

10. Bake according to **BAKING DIRECTIONS** given in the recipe. The given time is an estimate. It will vary depending on the type of cake pan used. Teflon cake pans take less time than metal cake pans. The given temperatures are for sea level. If baking over 5,000 feet above sea level, you may need to increase the oven temperature 15 to 25 degrees so that the cake will quickly set and not dry out. You also need to reduce baking time by 5 or 10 minutes because of the higher altitude (and temperature).

HOW TO FILL AND FROST A CAKE

Rather than have a separate frosting and filling section, we included recipes for frostings and fillings that go well with the given cake recipe. Make the filling and frosting according to the given recipe, then spread them on the cake as follows:

PREPARE TO FILL AND FROST
The cake needs to be room temperature.
Take your serving plate and line the edges with wax paper.
Put the rounded side of the cake on the plate.

Some bakers cut the rounded top off of the cake to make it sit flat on the plate. I leave the cake rounded. If it does not sit perfectly flat on the plate, the side frosting will cover any space at the bottom.

FILL THE CAKE
Place a cup of filling in the center of the bottom layer. Spread the filling out to within an inch of the edge. The weight of the next layer will spread the filling out to the edge. Place the next layer flat side down on the filling, with rounded side on the top of the cake. There's no harm in having the top of the cake with rounded edges. However, it you want a flat top, "straighten" it out by putting extra frosting around the top edge of the cake.

FROST THE CAKE
Use a spatula to coat the cake with frosting. Start with the sides, then top the cake with whatever frosting remains. Once frosted, remove the wax paper from under the cake.

WHITE CAKE

The White Cake is a versatile cake. It can be filled with preserves (raspberry, orange marmalade, apricot, cherry) and topped with any frosting. The cake pictured on page 56 has a raspberry filling and coconut frosting.

Spray two 9" cake pans. Preheat oven to 350°.
Follow steps 1-6 of the CAKE BAKING directions on page 58.

DRY INGREDIENTS

- ☐ 2/3 cup RICE FLOUR
- ☐ 2/3 cup TAPIOCA FLOUR
- ☐ 1 TBSP BAKING POWDER
- ☐ 1 tsp XANTHAN GUM
- ☐ 1/4 cup CORN STARCH
- ☐ 1/4 cup POTATO STARCH
- ☐ 1/4 tsp BAKING SODA
- ☐ 3/4 tsp SALT

LIQUID INGREDIENTS

- ☐ 1 cup MILK (whole or 2% fat)
- ☐ 1 1/2 tsp WHITE VINEGAR
- ☐ 1 tsp VANILLA

SHORTENING INGREDIENTS

- ☐ 3 TBSP BUTTER
- ☐ 1/3 cup LIGHT OLIVE OIL
- ☐ 1 cup SUGAR

Beat EGG MIXTURE till stiff.

EGG MIXTURE

- ☐ 4 EGG WHITES
- ☐ 1/2 tsp CREAM OF TARTAR

Alternate DRY and LIQUID INGREDIENTS (page 57), then fold in beaten EGG WHITES.

BAKING DIRECTIONS

Bake at 350° for 25 minutes or till the cake is golden brown and pulls away from the sides of the pan.

RASPBERRY COCONUT CAKE

Put PRESERVES in a bowl. Mash with a fork to an even spreading consistency.　☐　**1 cup RASPBERRY PRESERVES**

Use a spatula to spread the preserves on the cake.

Frost the top and sides of the cake with SEVEN MINUTE, or FLUFFY WHITE FROSTING, then press COCONUT FLAKES onto the frosting.　☐　**1 cup SWEETENED COCONUT FLAKES**

SEVEN MINUTE FROSTING

Combine the following ingredients in the top pot of a double broiler.

☐　**2 EGG WHITES**　　　　☐　**1/2 cup WATER**
☐　**1 1/3 cups SUGAR**　　　☐　**1 tsp SALT**
☐　**1 TBSP LIGHT CORN SYRUP**

Beat 1 minute. Meanwhile heat water in the bottom double broiler pot. Place the top pot over simmering (not boiling) water. Beat until the frosting holds its peak (about 6 minutes). Remove from heat. Add VANILLA and beat till stiff enough to spread.

☐　**1/2 tsp VANILLA**

The Seven Minute Frosting looks simple. Put the ingredients into a double broiler and beat with an electric mixer for 7 minutes. However, if you cook it too long or over too high a temperature, the results will disappoint. For an easy no-cook frosting, try the Fluffy White Frosting.

FLUFFY WHITE FROSTING

Put EGG WHITES and WATER in a large bowl. Stir 3 to 4 minutes with fork till the powder is absorbed.

☐　**1/4 cup DRIED EGG WHITES (JUST WHITES)**
☐　**1/2 cup WARM WATER**

Beat with an electric mixer till it forms peaks. Gradually add SUGAR and VANILLA. Beat till stiff enough to spread.

☐　**3 cups SIFTED POWDERED SUGAR**
☐　**1 tsp VANILLA**

YELLOW CAKE

Yellow cake with chocolate frosting is a classic. We went decadent, making a three layer cake with a double layer of chocolate and chocolate curls on top.

Spray cake pan(s). Preheat the oven to 350°.
Follow CAKE BAKING directions on page 58.

DRY INGREDIENTS
- ☐ 2/3 cup RICE FLOUR
- ☐ 2/3 cup TAPIOCA FLOUR
- ☐ 2 tsp BAKING POWDER
- ☐ 1 1/4 tsp XANTHAN GUM
- ☐ 2 tsp EGG REPLACER
- ☐ 1/3 cup CORN STARCH
- ☐ 1/3 cup POTATO STARCH
- ☐ 1 tsp BAKING SODA
- ☐ 3/4 tsp SALT

LIQUID INGREDIENTS
- ☐ 1 cup MILK (whole or 2% fat)
- ☐ 1 tsp VANILLA
- ☐ 1 1/2 tsp WHITE VINEGAR

SHORTENING INGREDIENTS
- ☐ 1/4 cup BUTTER
- ☐ 1/4 cup LIGHT OLIVE OIL
- ☐ 1 cup SUGAR

EGGS
- ☐ 3 EGGS + 1 EGG YOLK

BAKING DIRECTIONS
This recipe may be used for two 9" cake pans or three 8" cake pans, or a sheet cake pan.

Bake at 350° for 25 to 30 minutes.
Bake until the cake is golden brown and begins to pull away from the sides of the pan. To double check, insert a toothpick in the middle of the cake. It will come out clean once the cake is baked.

DOUBLE CHOCOLATE FROSTING

Beat the following ingredients till creamy.

☐ 1 1/2 cups BUTTER (3 sticks) (room temperature)
☐ 1 cup BAKING COCOA

Add the following and continue to beat for 3 minutes.

☐ 1 LARGE JAR (16 oz) MARSHMALLOW FLUFF
☐ 2 cups POWDERED SUGAR

Use two-thirds of the frosting to fill the layers and frost the cake (page 59). Cover the remaining frosting with plastic wrap.

Refrigerate the cake until the frosting is no longer tacky (2 hours or more), then add a second layer of frosting to the cake.

DECORATING THE CAKE

Chocolate curls make a nice finishing touch. The contrast of the dark chocolate curls and the light chocolate frosting is worth the extra effort.

CHOCOLATE CURLS

Melt CHOCOLATE in a double broiler over simmering water.

☐ 4 squares SEMI-SWEET BAKING CHOCOLATE

Pour the melted chocolate onto a clean cookie sheet. Spread out evenly to 9" X 9" square. Refrigerate a few minutes to harden the chocolate until it's no longer tacky. Make curls by scraping the chocolate in rows using a butter knife or thin metal spatula.

If the chocolate shaves instead of curling, it is too cold. Let it stand at room temperature for a while. If it's too soft to hold its shape, refrigerate until it is cool enough to form curls.

To hold their shape, store the curls in the refrigerator or freezer.

SPONGE CAKE

Sponge cake is perfect for a whipped cream cake. We included two recipes: a traditional round Strawberry Cream Cake (made with two cake pans), and a rectangular Banana Cream Cake (made with a cookie sheet).
Use the following recipe for either cake.

Line the cake pan(s) with parchment **(page 206)**.
Beat EGGS with the whisk attachment of an electric mixer till frothy. Add CREAM OF TARTAR and beat for 15 minutes.

☐ 4 EGGS (room temperature)
☐ 1/2 tsp CREAM OF TARTAR

SUGAR MIXTURE
Gradually add SUGAR and then VANILLA to the beaten EGGS.

☐ 3/4 cup SUGAR   ☐ 1 tsp VANILLA

Continue to beat for another 5 minutes.
Meanwhile, preheat oven to 350°.

Sift and mix DRY INGREDIENTS.
DRY INGREDIENTS
☐ 1 1/4 cup G-F CAKE FLOUR   ☐ 1/4 tsp SALT
☐ 2 tsp BAKING POWDER   ☐ 1 tsp XANTHAN GUM

Heat MILK to a simmer (page 208).

☐ 2/3 cup MILK (whole or 2% fat)

Fold sifted DRY INGREDIENTS into beaten EGG and SUGAR MIXTURE until fully blended. Stir in heated MILK till batter is of uniform consistency, i.e., no thick or thin areas.

BAKING DIRECTIONS
Bake at 350° for 20 minutes or until the cake is golden brown and begins to pull away from the sides of the pan. Allow the cake to cool in the baking pan before removing the parchment.

STRAWBERRY CREAM CAKE

Bake two Sponge Cakes using 9" cake pans.
Wash strawberries in cold water and cut off the stems.

☐ **2 cups (1 pint) STRAWBERRIES**

Save one or two strawberries for garnish. Cut the rest the into half inch slices. Place them in a bowl and cover with sugar.

☐ **3/4 cup SUGAR**

Let stand for 40 minutes, stirring once or twice.

Make WHIPPED CREAM using the following ingredients (page 210).

☐ **2 cups (1 pint) HEAVY CREAM**

☐ **3/4 cup SUGAR** ☐ **1 tsp VANILLA**

Assemble the cake by putting half of the strawberries and juice on the bottom cake layer. Put a layer of whipped cream on top of the strawberries. Put the second cake layer on top of the whipped cream and cover it with the rest of the strawberries and juice. Frost the top and sides of the cake with the remaining whipped cream and decorative strawberry.

BANANA CREAM CAKE

Bake a Sponge Cake using a cookie sheet (10" X 15" X 1 3/8").
When room temperature, cut down the middle of the 15" side of the pan forming two layers each 9" X 7 1/2".
Make WHIPPED CREAM using the above recipe.

Cut BANANAS into one inch circles. ☐ **6 BANANAS**
Put the sliced BANANAS in a bowl and sprinkle with juice.

☐ **1/2 cup ORANGE JUICE** ☐ **1 TBSP LEMON JUICE**

Assemble the cake by putting half the bananas and half the juice on one layer. Cover with half of the whipped cream. Put the second cake layer on top. Cover with the rest of the bananas and juice. Top with the remaining whipped cream.

CHOCOLATE CAKE

I don't know which tastes best — this dark chocolate cake or its dark chocolate frosting topped with white chocolate curls. One thing for sure, no one will know it's gluten free unless you tell them.

You can bake this cake in two 9" cake pans (as we did) or in three 8" cake pans or a single sheet cake pan (9" X 13").
Sift and mix DRY INGREDIENTS.

DRY INGREDIENTS
- ☐ 2 cups G-F CAKE FLOUR
- ☐ 3/4 cup BAKING COCOA
- ☐ 2 tsp BAKING POWDER
- ☐ 1 tsp BAKING SODA
- ☐ 1/2 tsp SALT
- ☐ 1 tsp XANTHAN GUM

Combine LIQUID INGREDIENTS in a bowl and set aside.

LIQUID INGREDIENTS
- ☐ 1 cup MILK
- ☐ 1/2 cup LIGHT OLIVE OIL
- ☐ 1 tsp VANILLA

EGG MIXTURE
- ☐ 2 EGGS + 1 EGG WHITE
- ☐ 1 1/4 cup SUGAR

Beat EGGS with the whisk attachment of an electric mixer for 15 minutes. Gradually add SUGAR and beat for another 5 minutes.
Start to heat WATER ☐ 3/4 cup BOILING WATER

Alternate DRY INGREDIENTS and LIQUID INGREDIENTS into EGG MIXTURE (page 57). Stir in BOILING WATER till batter is of uniform consistency, i.e., no thick or thin areas.

BAKING DIRECTIONS
Bake at 350° FOR 25 minutes.

DARK CHOCOLATE FROSTING

This recipe makes enough frosting for a three layer cake. You may have frosting left over if you make a two layer cake. If so, refrigerate the cake till the frosting is firm, then give it a second layer of frosting.

Beat the following with an electric mixer in the order given.
- ☐ 3/4 cup BUTTER (room temperature)
- ☐ 1 cup BAKING COCOA
- ☐ 1 cup POWDERED SUGAR
- ☐ 1/2 cup MILK
- ☐ 1 tsp VANILLA

Gradually add POWDERED SUGAR till spreading consistency
- ☐ 4 to 4 1/2 cups POWDERED SUGAR

WHITE CHOCOLATE CURLS

Melt WHITE CHOCOLATE in a double broiler over simmering water (page 205).
- ☐ 4 squares BAKER'S WHITE CHOCOLATE

Pour the melted chocolate onto a clean cookie sheet. Spread evenly to 9" X 9" square. Put the cookie sheet in the refrigerator a few minutes until your finger leaves a slight mark on the chocolate, but not a depression. Scrape the chocolate in a row using a butter knife or thin metal spatula.

White chocolate goes to room temperature faster than does dark chocolate so you may need to return the cookie tray to the refrigerator until it is hard enough to form curls.

If you are not ready to decorate the cake, put the curls on a plate, or in a plastic bag, and refrigerate till ready to use.

ANGEL FOOD CAKE

Angel Food Cake is easy to make. The only problem is what to do with the left over egg yolks. The INGREDIENT INDEX has two listings that help: EGG YOLKS ONLY listing recipes that use egg yolks and no whites and EGG YOLKS, EXTRA listing recipes that require extra egg yolks.

THE TUBE PAN
Start with a clean, ungreased, 9" X 5" Angle Food pan (a tube pan with a removable base). A spec of grease will prevent the egg whites from rising properly, so wipe the tube pan, mixing bowl, beaters and spatula with a paper towel dampened with WHITE VINEGAR.

Bring EGG WHITES to room temperature (page 205).
Preheat oven to 375º.

Sift DRY INGREDIENTS together 3 times, then mix with a spoon.
DRY INGREDIENTS
- ☐ 1/2 cup POTATO STARCH
- ☐ 1 cup POWDERED SUGAR
- ☐ 1/2 cup CORN STARCH
- ☐ 1/4 tsp SALT

Beat EGG WHITES till foamy, then add CREAM OF TARTAR and continue to beat until it holds soft peaks.
- ☐ 1 1/2 cup EGG WHITES (10 to 12 eggs)
- ☐ 1 1/2 tsp CREAM OF TARTAR

Add SUGAR, a tablespoon at a time. Continue to beat till it forms stiff peaks, then add VANILLA.
- ☐ 2/3 cup SUGAR
- ☐ 1 tsp VANILLA

Gradually fold DRY INGREDIENTS into the beaten EGG mixture. Pour batter into the tube pan.
Cut batter through with a knife or spatula to break large air bubbles. Smooth the top of the batter with a spatula.

ANGEL FOOD CAKE

BAKING DIRECTIONS

Bake at 375^0 for 20 minute. Reduce heat to 350^0 and bake another 20 minutes until it is golden brown and pulls away from the sides of the pan.

Cool to room temperature before removing from the baking pan.

TOP WITH FRUIT

Fruit is a natural topping for the Angel Food Cake. A Berry Topping, made with strawberries, was used on the Angel Food Cake pictured on page 56. It was garnished with bananas and blueberries.

BERRY TOPPING

The following Berry Topping recipe can be made with strawberries, cherries, blueberries, raspberries or even cranberries.

Mix the following ingredients together in a small saucepan.
- ☐ 1 TBSP LEMON JUICE
- ☐ 1 cup WATER
- ☐ 2 TBSP CORN STARCH
- ☐ 1/8 tsp SALT
- ☐ 2/3 cup sugar

Cook over a medium heat until it comes to a rolling boil.

Add the fruit and cook a few minutes until it returns to a boil and the liquid is fruit colored.

FRUIT   ☐ 2 cups BERRIES (fresh or frozen)

Cool, then pour over a serving of the Angel Food Cake.

THE BASIC CAKE   *69*

RAISIN SPICE CAKE

The SPICE CAKE is a natural to bake in a Bundt pan. It holds its shape and does not require a filling.

Soak RAISINS in a cup of WARM WATER for 20 minutes.
- ☐ 2/3 cup RAISINS

Spray a fluted Bundt pan.
Preheat the oven to 350°.

Follow CAKE BAKING directions on page 58.

DRY INGREDIENTS
- ☐ 2 cups G-F CAKE FLOUR
- ☐ 1/2 tsp SALT
- ☐ 1 1/2 tsp XANTHAN GUM
- ☐ 1 TBSP BAKING POWDER
- ☐ 1 1/2 tsp CINNAMON
- ☐ 1/2 tsp NUTMEG
- ☐ 1/4 tsp CLOVES
- ☐ 1 tsp ALLSPICE

LIQUID INGREDIENTS
- ☐ 1 cup MILK

SHORTENING INGREDIENTS
- ☐ 1/2 cup BUTTER
- ☐ 1/2 cup SUGAR
- ☐ 1/2 cup BROWN SUGAR

EGGS
- ☐ 3 EGGS + 1 EGG WHITE

Drain RAISINS, pat them dry with a paper towel and then fold them into the batter.

RAISIN SPICE CAKE

BAKING DIRECTIONS

Bake at 350° for 40 minutes or till slightly brown and pulls away from side of pan.

When the cake is room temperature, frost it with BUTTER CREAM FROSTING, then sprinkle WALNUTS over the top and sides of the cake.

☐ 1 cup CHOPPED WALNUTS

BUTTER CREAM FROSTING

Bring BUTTER and CREAM CHEESE to room temperature (page 205).

Beat the following ingredients in an electric mixer using the paddle attachment.

☐ 1/4 cup BUTTER
☐ 1 package (8 oz) CREAM CHEESE
☐ 1 tsp VANILLA

Add the POWDERED SUGAR a cup at a time beating after each addition until the frosting is spreading consistency..

☐ 5 to 6 cups SIFTED POWDERED SUGAR

POUND CAKE

Nothing more basic than Pound Cake. Eat it plain, with a Lemon Glaze, or use it in other recipes, such as the Trifle described in the top paragraph of page 170.

Spray a loaf pan (5" X 9" X 3"). Preheat the oven to 350°.
Follow steps 1 - 6 of CAKE BAKING directions on page 58.

DRY INGREDIENTS

- ☐ 1/2 cup RICE FLOUR
- ☐ 1/2 cup TAPIOCA FLOUR
- ☐ 2 tsp EGG REPLACER
- ☐ 1 tsp XANTHAN GUM
- ☐ 2 tsp BAKING POWDER
- ☐ 1/3 cup CORN STARCH
- ☐ 1/3 cup POTATO STARCH
- ☐ 3/4 tsp SALT
- ☐ 1/8 tsp NUTMEG
- ☐ 1/2 tsp BAKING SODA

LIQUID INGREDIENTS

- ☐ 1/2 cup BUTTERMILK
- ☐ 1 tsp VANILLA

SHORTENING INGREDIENTS

- ☐ 1/2 cup BUTTER
- ☐ 1 cup SUGAR

Beat EGGS till stiff.   ☐ 3 EGGS
Alternate DRY and LIQUID INGREDIENTS into shortening (page 57). Fold in beaten EGGS (page 207).

BAKING DIRECTIONS

Bake at 325° for 50 minutes until a toothpick inserted in the middle comes out clean. Let cool in the loaf pan.

===

LEMON GLAZE

Before squeezing the juice, make the LEMON RIND (page 211).
Mix the following ingredients together till smooth.

- ☐ 1 cup POWDERED SUGAR
- ☐ 1 tsp LEMON RIND   ☐ 1 1/2 TBSP LEMON JUICE

Pour the LEMON GLAZE over the cake or over each serving.

Favorite Desserts Made Gluten Free

Special Event Cake

The Sheet Cake 76

Pineapple Upside-Down Cake 78

Carrot Cake 80

Red Velvet Cake 82

German Chocolate Cupcake 85

Tres Leches 86

Orange Chiffon Cake 88

Mini Fruit Cupcakes 90

CHOOSING THE RIGHT CAKE

The most important part of baking a cake for a special event is the thinking part. You need to ask yourself:

How many people will my cake need to serve?
i.e., how big a cake do I need?

Do I have cake pans large enough to bake the cake?
You can buy large cake pans, but then there's the problem of storing them. You may not need a large pan again for a long time. Luckily, there are inexpensive foil (disposable) cake pans available in super markets.

Will the cake need to be refrigerated?
If yes, do I have space in the refrigerator?

Have I baked this cake before?
This is not the best time to experiment with a new recipe.

How am I going to decorate the cake?
With each cake recipe we suggest simple ways to decorate the cake to make it look as good as it tastes. Look at cake decoration sets in the supermarket for other ideas.

What shape cake pan shall I use?
There are decorative tubed pans, tiered baking pans and formed cake pans on the market — all sure to please your guests. The castle shaped cake pictured on the previous page is not only for little ones but for adults who love the medieval era. Decorative tubed pans and formed cake pans need a cake that can be easily removed from the mold. Pound Cake, Chocolate Cake, Red Velvet Cake, Spice Cake work well. Sponge Cake, Angel Food Cake, Chiffon Cake do not.

THE GRADUATION CAKE

The Graduation Cake is the perfect sheet cake. Plenty of room to write the name of the class and congrats to the happy graduate. One problem is finding a serving platter large enough to accommodate the size of a sheet cake (9" X 13" X 2 "). An easy solution is to bake and serve the cake in the baking pan. To give the cake a party look, bake it in a Hefty Foil Sheet Cake Pan. When room temperature, cut each corner of the pan (top to bottom) with a pair of kitchen scissors. Lay the foil sides down flat, cover them in wax paper, frost the cake, remove the wax paper, then cover the cut foil with doilies. See Graduation Cake on page 73.

HOW TO WRITE ON A CAKE

Writing on a cake is not as simple as it looks. You need something to write with. You could make your own colored sugar mix; however, if you are an infrequent baker it's best to buy a tube of **DECORATIVE GEL** at the food store rather than struggle to make a Gel with the right color and consistency.

Next you need a surface that will support the Gel. The Smooth Frosting on page 77 does the job. The Double Chocolate Frosting on page 63 works well for a chocolate cake.

Now you're all set to write — maybe. The problem is spacing. You start to write *Congratulations PRISCILLA* only to run out of space *Congratulations PRIS. . .* Practice is the answer. Once you take off the Gel cap, you will see a rounded tip. The tip needs to be cut in order to squeeze out the Gel. Before cutting, use the tip to practice writing. If you mess up, smooth the frosting with a spatula and try again. Once the writing is to your liking, cut off the tip and use the Gel to fill in the groves made with the rounded tip.

THE SHEET CAKE

Preheat oven to 350°.
Spray (or butter) the bottom of a sheet cake pan (9" X 13" X 2").

Use and electric mixer to beat EGG INGREDIENTS for 15 minutes until thick and lemon colored.

EGG INGREDIENTS ☐ 3 EGGS + 1 EGG WHITE
☐ 1/2 tsp CREAM OF TARTAR

Meanwhile, sift and mix DRY INGREDIENTS.

DRY INGREDIENTS
☐ 2 cups G-F CAKE FLOUR
☐ 1 1/2 tsp XANTHAN GUM   ☐ 1/2 tsp SALT
☐ 1 TBSP BAKING POWDER   ☐ 1 tsp BAKING SODA

Cream SHORTENING INGREDIENTS.

SHORTENING INGREDIENTS
☐ 1 cup SUGAR   ☐ 2/3 cup BUTTER
☐ 1 tsp VANILLA

Alternate DRY INGREDIENTS and MILK into SHORTENING INGREDIENTS (page 57).

MILK   ☐ 1 1/2 cup MILK (whole or 2% fat)

Fold beaten EGGS into the batter (page 207).

BAKING DIRECTIONS
Bake at 350° for 35 minutes or till golden brown and pulls away from edge of the pan.

Once the cake is room temperature, top it with peaches (fresh or canned) and then frost the cake with whipped cream. Another approach is to bake fruit into the cake as with the Pineapple Upside-down Sheet Cake on the next page.

PINEAPPLE UPSIDE-DOWN CAKE

Preheat the oven to 350⁰. Liberally spread BUTTER on bottom and sides of a sheet cake pan (9" X 13" X 2").

☐ **3 TBSP BUTTER (or MARGARINE)**

Sprinkle BROWN SUGAR on top of the BUTTER.

☐ **1 cup BROWN SUGAR**

DRAIN PINEAPPLES and CHERRIES

☐ **10 PINEAPPLE SLICES (20 oz can)**

☐ **12 MARASCHINO CHERRIES**

Reserve 2 PINEAPPLE SLICES and 4 CHERRIES to decorate the top of the cake. Place the 8 remaining PINEAPPLE slices on top of the BROWN SUGAR. Place a cherry in the middle of each slice. Place PECAN HALVES in the spaces surrounding the PINEAPPLE SLICES.   ☐ **10 PECAN HALVES**

Make a SHEET CAKE batter using the recipe on the last page. Pour it over the fruit and nuts and bake at 350⁰ for 15 minutes. Reduce heat to 325⁰ and continue baking for 25 to 30 minutes or till golden brown and the cake pulls away from the sides.

SMOOTH FROSTING

Beat the following ingredients in the order given.

☐ **5 TBSP CRISCO**

☐ **4 TBSP BUTTER (room temperature)**

☐ **1/3 cup EVAPORATED MILK**

☐ **1 1/2 tsp VANILLA**

Gradually beat in the SIFTED SUGAR to spreading consistency.

☐ **up to 6 cups SIFTED POWDERED SUGAR**

When the cake is at room temperature use a spatula to spread the frosting over the cake.

THE DINNER PARTY

SQUARE PINEAPPLE UPSIDE-DOWN CAKE

The square Pineapple Upside-Down cake is great for a smaller crowd, perhaps as dessert for Sunday dinner. You do not need to frost the cake. It tastes great by itself.

Preheat oven to 350°. Liberally BUTTER the sides and bottom of a square pan (8" X 8" X 2")
- ☐ 2 TBSP BUTTER (or MARGARINE)

Sprinkle the bottom of the pan with SUGAR.
- ☐ 1/2 cup LIGHT BROWN SUGAR

Drain PINEAPPLES and CHERRIES. Arrange on top of sugar.
- ☐ 4 PINEAPPLE SLICES (one 8 oz can)
- ☐ 5 MARASCHINO CHERRIES

Mix the batter using the SHEET CAKE directions on page 76.

EGG INGREDIENTS
- ☐ 2 EGGS + 1 EGG WHITE
- ☐ 1/2 tsp CREAM OF TARTAR

DRY INGREDIENTS
- ☐ 1 cup G-F CAKE FLOUR
- ☐ 2 TBSP CORN STARCH
- ☐ 1/4 tsp SALT
- ☐ 1 TBSP BAKING POWDER
- ☐ 1 tsp XANTHAN GUM

SHORTENING INGREDIENTS
- ☐ 2/3 cup SUGAR
- ☐ 1/3 cup BUTTER
- ☐ 3/4 tsp VANILLA

MILK
- ☐ 1 cup MILK (whole or 2% fat)

BAKING DIRECTIONS
Bake at 350° for 35 minutes or til the cake is golden brown and pulls away from the sides of the pan.
Let cool in pan before turning upside-down on the cake platter.

THE WEDDING OR ANNIVERSARY

The traditional wedding or anniversary cake is tiered. I used to have a three tiered cake pan set with four cake pans each fitting one inside the other. Over the years they disappeared. I have no idea where. I thought it would be an easy thing to replace the set.
Not.

None of my local haunts (supermarkets, stores with kitchen departments, etc.) carried tier sets. A quick trip to the Internet and I found any tier set imaginable — 4 tiers, 5 tiers, square tiers, scalloped tiers. When I added shipping and handling it came to more than I wanted to spend just to take a picture of a tiered cake for this book.

So I improvised. I used a 10" spring form pan, an 8" cake pan and a 6" decorative Bundt pan for the top. I did not fill the spring form to the top, but used as much batter as if I were making a 10" layer cake.

I used a Carrot Cake recipe because it is a dense cake and holds up nicely to the weight of more than one layer. I frosted the cake with Butter Cream and topped it with a cake decoration bride and groom. I sprinkled red decorative sugar to accent the tiers (see page 73).

CARROT CAKE

Use a food processor to grate 6 or 7 carrots that have been washed and scraped (or peeled).

Mix the CARROT INGREDIENTS in a bowl and set aside.

CARROT INGREDIENTS
- ☐ 2 cups SHREDDED CARROTS
- ☐ 2/3 cup CHOPPED WALNUTS
- ☐ 2/3 cup RAISINS

Preheat the oven to 350°. Spray the cake pans.

Mix the batter using the CAKE BAKING directions on page 58.

DRY INGREDIENTS
- ☐ 2 cups G-F ALL PURPOSE FLOUR
- ☐ 2 tsp BAKING POWDER
- ☐ 1/2 tsp BAKING SODA
- ☐ 1 1/2 tsp XANTHAN GUM
- ☐ 1/2 tsp SALT
- ☐ 1 tsp CINNAMON
- ☐ 1/4 tsp GINGER

LIQUID INGREDIENT   ☐   1/4 cup MILK

SHORTENING MIX
- ☐ 1/2 cup LIGHT OLIVE OIL
- ☐ 1/2 cup SUGAR
- ☐ 2/3 cup LIGHT BROWN SUGAR

EGGS   ☐ 4 EGGS

Once the batter is mixed, fold in the CARROT INGREDIENTS.

CARROT CAKE

BAKING DIRECTIONS

Bake at 350^0 until the cake pulls away from the sides of the pan. Different size pans take different baking times. A 6" pan takes 25 minutes. An 8" takes 30 minutes. A 10" pan, 35 minutes.

Once the cake is room temperature fill the layers with PINEAPPLE FILLING.

PINEAPPLE FILLING

Put the contents of a can of Pineapple (juice and all) into a saucepan.

- ☐ 1 can (20 oz) CRUSHED PINEAPPLE

Add the following ingredients and stir till blended.

- ☐ 1/8 tsp SALT
- ☐ 1/4 cup CORN STARCH
- ☐ 1/3 cup SUGAR

Cook over low heat until mixture comes to a boil.
Cool, then spread between the cake layers.

BUTTER CREAM FROSTING

Use the BUTTER CREAM FROSTING recipe on page 71 to frost the cake.

THE BIRTHDAY PARTY

Planning a birthday cake is easy. You know what cake the birthday person likes best. It is a simple matter to put the age on the cake with a confectionery number found in supermarkets. This recipe is for a Red Velvet Cake. It was baked in a "castle" pan, but the same recipe will make two 9" layer cakes or three 8" layer cakes.

RED VELVET CAKE

Preheat oven to 350°. Spray the cake pan.
Follow CAKE BAKING directions on page 58.

DRY INGREDIENTS
- ☐ 2 cups G-F CAKE FLOUR
- ☐ 1 tsp BAKING SODA
- ☐ 1 1/2 tsp XANTHAN GUM
- ☐ 1/4 cup BAKING COCOA
- ☐ 2 tsp BAKING POWDER
- ☐ 1/2 TSP SALT

LIQUID INGREDIENTS
- ☐ 1 1/3 cup BUTTERMILK
- ☐ 1 tsp VANILLA

SHORTENING INGREDIENTS
- ☐ 1 1/2 cup SUGAR
- ☐ 1/2 cup LIGHT OLIVE OIL
- ☐ 4 TBSP RED FOOD COLORING (2 one oz bottles)

EGGS   ☐ 3 EGGS

BAKING DIRECTIONS
Bake at 350° for 40 minutes or till the cake pulls away from the sides of the pan. Cool the cake in the pan.

See next page for the CHERRY FILLING and VANILLA GLAZE.

RED VELVET CAKE

Many form pans, including the castle pan used to bake the cake pictured on page 73, are tubed pans i.e., they have a hole in the middle. There are any number of ways to fill the space, with ice cream the easiest and most popular. The following Cherry Filling goes well with most cakes.

CHERRY FILLING

Whisk the SYRUP INGREDIENTS together in a small saucepan.
SYRUP INGREDIENTS
- ☐ 1 TBSP LEMON JUICE
- ☐ 3 TBSP CORN STARCH
- ☐ 2/3 cup SUGAR
- ☐ 1 cup WATER
- ☐ 1/8 tsp SALT

Cook over a medium heat until the syrup comes to a rolling boil. Add the CHERRIES and cook a few minutes until the syrup is fruit colored.   ☐ **12 oz FROZEN CHERRIES**

Cool to room temperature, then fill the cake.

Frost the cake with a Vanilla Glaze to accent the outline of the castle.

VANILLA GLAZE

Beat the following ingredients together till smooth.
- ☐ 2 cups SIFTED POWDERED SUGAR
- ☐ 1 tsp VANILLA
- ☐ 2 TBSP MILK

The Glaze should be thin enough to pour, yet thick enough to "stick."

Line the cake platter with wax paper (page 59), then pour the Glaze over the cake.

THE PICNIC OR BEACH PARTY

You're having a party. It isn't a milestone event. Just a gathering — maybe a picnic, or beach party. You want a dessert that can be carried to a picnic or beach party. Cupcakes are a good choice. They keep fresh for hours. You can bake them the day before and cover them with plastic wrap. This recipe is for 24 German Chocolate Cupcakes. This same recipe works for a sheet cake or for a three layer German Chocolate Cake. Any way you make this cake, it will be a crowd pleaser.

COCONUT PECAN FROSTING

The thing that makes a chocolate cake a German Chocolate Cake is its distinctive Coconut Pecan Frosting. This frosting needs a few hours in the refrigerator to set, so you may want to make the frosting the day before.

Mix the following ingredients over medium heat stirring until it comes to a rolling boil.

- ☐ 1 cup EVAPORATED MILK
- ☐ 1/2 cup LIGHT BROWN SUGAR
- ☐ 1/2 cup SUGAR ☐ 2 EGG YOLKS (lightly beaten)
- ☐ 1/2 cup BUTTER ☐ 1/8 tsp SALT

Remove from heat and add the following

- ☐ 1 1/2 cups SWEETENED FLAKED COCONUT
- ☐ 1 cup PECANS (coarsely chopped)
- ☐ 1 tsp VANILLA

Cool, then refrigerate. Stir every half hour until it is spreading consistency.

NOTE: This recipe is enough to frost 24 cupcakes. If you wish to fill the cupcakes as we did (see page 73), you need to double the recipe.

GERMAN CHOCOLATE CAKE

Spray baking pan(s). Preheat oven to 350⁰.

Heat CHOCOLATE INGREDIENTS in the micro, mixing with a spoon at 30 seconds intervals until smooth, then set aside.

CHOCOLATE INGREDIENTS
- ☐ 3 1/2 squares SEMISWEET BAKING CHOCOLATE (chopped into quarters)
- ☐ 1/2 cup WATER

Mix the batter using the CAKE BAKING directions on page 58.

DRY INGREDIENTS
- ☐ 2 cups G-F CAKE FLOUR
- ☐ 1 1/2 tsp XANTHAN GUM
- ☐ 1 tsp BAKING SODA
- ☐ 2 tsp BAKING POWDER
- ☐ 1/2 tsp SALT

LIQUID INGREDIENTS
- ☐ 1 cup BUTTERMILK   ☐ 1 tsp VANILLA

SHORTENING INGREDIENTS
- ☐ 1/2 cup BUTTER   ☐ 1 1/4 cup SUGAR

EGGS
☐ 4 EGGS

Fold the CHOCOLATE MIX into the batter until blended.

BAKING DIRECTIONS
Bake at 350⁰ for 30 minutes or until a toothpick inserted in the middle comes out clean.

Frost with COCONUT PECAN FROSTING using recipe on the last page.

THE INFORMAL PARTY

Tres Leches stands for "Three Milks," a milk mixture that is poured over the cake after it is baked. It takes a day to be absorbed into the cake. This is a great party cake, not only for the convenience of baking it the day before, but for the plaudits you are sure to receive from your grateful guests.

TRES LECHES

Bring EGGS and MILK to room temperature. Preheat the oven to 350°. Butter a sheet cake pan (9" X 13" X 2").

☐ 1 TBSP BUTTER (or MARGARINE)

Beat EGG YOLK MIXTURE with the whisk attachment to an electric mixer for 15 minutes.

EGG YOLK INGREDIENTS

☐ 5 EGG YOLKS ☐ 3/4 cup SUGAR

Meanwhile, sift and mix the DRY INGREDIENTS.

DRY INGREDIENTS

☐ 1 cup G-F CAKE FLOUR ☐ 2 tsp BAKING POWDER
☐ 3/4 tsp XANTHAN GUM ☐ 1/4 tsp SALT

EGG WHITE INGREDIENTS

Beat EGG WHITES, gradually add CREAM OF TARTAR and SUGAR. Beat till glossy with firm peaks. Don't over beat.

☐ 5 EGG WHITES ☐ 1/2 tsp CREAM OF TARTAR
☐ 1/4 cup SUGAR

LIQUID INGREDIENTS

☐ 1/3 cup MILK ☐ 1/2 tsp VANILLA

Alternate DRY INGREDIENTS and LIQUID INGREDIENTS into the beaten EGG YOLKS (page 57).
Fold the beaten EGG WHITES into the batter (page 207).

TRES LECHES

BAKING DIRECTIONS

Bake at 350° for 25 minutes until it is golden brown and begins to pull away from the sides of the pan.

Let cake cool to room temperature in the baking pan.

Stir the MILK INGREDIENTS until blended.

MILK INGREDIENTS

- ☐ 3/4 cup EVAPORATED MILK
- ☐ 3/4 cup SWEETENED CONDENSED MILK
- ☐ 3/4 cup HEAVY CREAM
- ☐ 1 tsp VANILLA

Pierce the cake with a large 2 prong cooking fork. Make 7 or 8 rows lengthwise. Pierce to the bottom, but do not tear the cake. Pour half of the MILK INGREDIENTS slowly over the cake. Wait a few minutes then gently pour the rest over the cake. Refrigerate the cake overnight. Top cake with MERINGUE FROSTING.

MERINGUE FROSTING

Heat SYRUP in a small sauce pan until it reaches the soft ball stage (page 209).

SYRUP   ☐ 1/4 cup WATER   ☐ 3/4 cup SUGAR

Meanwhile, beat EGG WHITE MIXTURE to soft peaks.

EGG WHITE INGREDIENTS

- ☐ 3 EGG WHITES   ☐ 1/2 tsp CREAM OF TARTAR

Add sugar and beat to stiff peaks.

- ☐ 2 TBSP SUGAR

Continue beating the EGG WHITE INGREDIENTS while slowly dribbling in the hot SYRUP.

Frost the cake and refrigerate it for at least an hour before serving.

THE SHOWER CAKE

The Orange Chiffon Cake is an easy cake to make and to decorate. It can be baked in a Bundt pan, filled with fruit, and topped with a glaze, or (as pictured on page 73) cut in half, filled and frosted. Add party favor umbrellas and you have a Wedding Shower or Baby Shower Cake.

ORANGE CHIFFON CAKE

Spray a 10" Bundt pan. Preheat oven to 325°.
Sift and mix DRY INGREDIENTS.

DRY INGREDIENTS
- ☐ 1 cup RICE FLOUR
- ☐ 1/4 cup TAPIOCA FLOUR
- ☐ 1 TBSP BAKING POWDER
- ☐ 1 tsp XANTHAN GUM
- ☐ 1/4 cup CORN STARCH
- ☐ 1/4 cup POTATO STARCH
- ☐ 1 tsp SALT

LIQUID INGREDIENTS
- ☐ 3/4 cup ORANGE JUICE
- ☐ 2 tsp ORANGE RIND

Grate the rind (page 211), then squeeze the juice from 2 or 3 NAVEL ORANGES and set aside.

Beat EGG WHITE INGREDIENTS till soft peaks form.

EGG WHITE INGREDIENTS
- ☐ 7 EGG WHITES
- ☐ 1/2 tsp CREAM OF TARTAR

Gradually add SUGAR and beat till very stiff.
- ☐ 1/2 cup POWDERED SUGAR

Beat SHORTENING INGREDIENTS in a large bowl till creamy.

SHORTENING INGREDIENTS
- ☐ 2 1/2 TBSP BUTTER
- ☐ 5 EGG YOLKS
- ☐ 1/3 cup LIGHT OLIVE OIL
- ☐ 1 cup SUGAR

Alternate DRY and LIQUID INGREDIENTS into the SHORTENING INGREDIENTS (page 57).
Fold the beaten EGG WHITES into the batter (page 207).

ORANGE CHIFFON CAKE

BAKING DIRECTIONS

Pour the batter into a sprayed 10" Bundt pan.

Bake at 325° for 55 to 60 minutes or till golden brown and a toothpick, inserted in the middle, comes out clean.

Let cake cool to room temperature in the Bundt pan.

DECORATING THE CAKE

Once the cake is at room temperature, remove it from the pan and put it rounded side up on a cake platter lined with wax paper. Cut the cake in half horizontally (page 208).

Spread APRICOT PRESERVES on the bottom layer of the cake.

☐ 1 cup APRICOT PRESERVES

Drain a can of MANDARIN ORANGES

☐ 1 can (8.25 oz) MANDARIN ORANGES.

Pat ORANGES dry on a paper towel. Place the MANDARIN ORANGES on top of the APRICOT PRESERVES, then cover with the top layer of the cake.

ORANGE FROSTING

Make ZEST from 2 ORANGES (page 211), then squeeze the juice from the orange.

Use an electric mixer to beat the following ingredients together.

☐ 3 TBSP BUTTER (or MARGARINE)
☐ 1/4 cup ORANGE JUICE

Gradually beat in the POWDERED SUGAR until the frosting is spreading consistency.

☐ 3 1/2 - 4 cups POWDERED SUGAR

Frost the cake, then decorate with ORANGE ZEST and party favor umbrellas.

☐ 1/4 cup ORANGE ZEST

THE HOLIDAY PARTY

MINI FRUIT CUPCAKES

Our Colonial ancestors made fruit cake as a holiday treat. To them, candied fruit in the middle of the winter was a luxury. Times (and tastes) have changed. For most of us a slice of fruit cake is too rich. A morsel sized mini cupcake is just right. This is perfect holiday dessert. You can bake it days ahead of time and have it ready any time guests drop in.

Preheat oven to 325°. Spray 2 mini cupcake pans or place cupcake liners in the cups.

Blend FRUIT MIXTURE together and set aside.

FRUIT MIXTURE

- ☐ 1 cup MIXED CANDIED FRUIT (chopped)
- ☐ 1 cup RAISINS   ☐ 1 cup WALNUT PIECES

Sift and mix DRY INGREDIENTS.

DRY INGREDIENTS

- ☐ 1 1/4 cup G-F CAKE FLOUR   ☐ 1/2 tsp SALT
- ☐ 1 tsp XANTHAN GUM   ☐ 1 tsp BAKING POWDER

Use an electric mixer to beat SHORTENING INGREDIENTS until light and fluffy.

SHORTENING INGREDIENTS

- ☐ 6 TBSP BUTTER (room temperature)
- ☐ 1/4 cup DARK BROWN SUGAR   ☐ 1/4 cup SUGAR
- ☐ 1 1/2 tsp RUM EXTRACT   ☐ 2 EGGS

Add DRY INGREDIENTS to SHORTENING MIX and stir till smooth. Fold in FRUIT MIXTURE.

BAKING DIRECTIONS

Divide batter evenly into two mini cup cake pans (12 per pan). Bake at 325° for 20 minutes or till golden brown.

Cheesecake

You can make a good cheesecake without much effort (see the French Cheesecake recipe on page 98 and the Ricotta Cheesecake recipe on page 100). New York style cheesecake has a smooth top, no cracked or sinking crust. As you will see on the next page, to make a *perfect* New York style cheesecake takes time and equipment — but it's well worth the effort.

New York Style Cheesecake 94

New York Style
Marble Cheesecake 96

French Cheesecake   98

Ricotta Cheesecake   100

HOW TO MAKE NY STYLE CHEESECAKE

THE EQUIPMENT

▶ AN ACCURATE OVEN — NOT CONVECTION.

You need an accurate oven. Check the accuracy of the oven with an oven thermometer. If your oven has a convection option, turn it off. The moving air may bake the cake too quickly causing the top to sink when it cools.

▶ 8" SPRINGFORM PAN WRAPPED IN HEAVY DUTY FOIL.

The recipe on page 94 makes an 8" cheesecake, so you need an 8" springform pan. The baking pan will be placed in a pan of hot water to make the cake bake evenly. To keep the water from seeping into the cake, the pan needs to be wrapped in foil.

THE FOIL WRAP

Tear off a 15" sheet of heavy duty aluminum foil. Put the pan in the center of the sheet and wrap the foil up the sides. Tuck the 4 corners over the side of the pan to secure it in place. Trim the 4 corners with a scissor so that they do not extend more than an inch into the springform pan.

BUTTER THE PAN

Butter the bottom and sides of the springform pan using two tablespoons of room temperature butter.

▶ A WATER BATH PAN

Any pan that is larger than the springform pan, and with sides as high, can serve as water bath pan. The Hefty Chicken Roasting 10" X 10" foil pan works well, provided it is placed it on a cookie sheet for stability and ease of handling.

HOW TO MAKE NY STYLE CHEESECAKE

Once the equipment is assembled and the ingredients at room temperature (page 205), you're ready to bake.

MAKE THE CRUST

Make the crust using the given recipe. The crust is baked in the foil lined springform pan. The water bath pan is used only for the cheesecake. The water bath needs to be boiling hot, so start heating the water as you put the crust into the oven. Once the crust is baked, remove it from the oven. Leave the oven on while you mix the batter.

MIX THE BATTER

Put one package of cream cheese in an electric mixer with paddle attachment. Start on low speed. Add the corn starch and a quarter of a cup of sugar, then add the rest of the cream cheese. Increase to medium speed and add the remaining sugar and vanilla. Add eggs one at a time and finally the heavy cream. Pour the batter over the baked crust.

Pull out the oven rack. Place the springform pan into the water bath pan and then on to the oven rack. Pour the boiling water into the water bath pan. Push the rack back into the oven and begin to bake.

BAKE THE CAKE

Keep the oven door closed for the first half hour. Turn on the oven light if you wish to see how the cake is doing. If you open the door before it has time to set, it may fall. The cake is baked when the top is light brown and the center set. Gently lift the cake out of its water bath and place it on a wire rack to cool. Do not move the cake for at least two hours; then remove the foil, but do not remove the cake from the springform pan. Cover the cake loosely with plastic wrap and refrigerate overnight.

NEW YORK STYLE CHEESECAKE

There are variations of New York Style cheese cake. Some have a sour cream topping. Others, like this cake, are served with powdered sugar or with a fruit sauce.

SPONGE CRUST

Prepare an 8" springform pan (page 92).
Preheat oven to 350°.
Mix DRY INGREDIENTS in a small bowl.

DRY INGREDIENTS

☐ 1/4 cup G-F CAKE FLOUR   ☐ 3/4 tsp BAKING POWDER
☐ 1/8 tsp SALT

EGG YOLK MIXTURE

Beat EGG YOLKS with an electric mixer for 3 minutes.
☐ 2 EGG YOLKS
Gradually beat in SUGAR and continue to beat 5 more minutes.
☐ 2 TBSP SUGAR

EGG WHITE MIXTURE

Clean beaters, then beat EGG WHITES with CREAM OF TARTAR
till firm.   ☐ 2 EGG WHITES   ☐ 1/4 tsp CREAM OF TARTAR
Beat in SUGAR   ☐ 2 TBSP SUGAR
Continue beating till stiff.

Mix DRY INGREDIENTS into EGG YOLK MIXTURE.
Blend in BUTTER and VANILLA.
☐ 2 TBSP MELTED BUTTER   ☐ 3/4 tsp VANILLA
Fold the EGG WHITE MIXTURE into the batter.
Pour into the 8" foil lined springform pan.

BAKING DIRECTIONS

Bake at 350° for 15 minutes or until it is golden brown around the edge and the center springs back when touched. Remove from the oven and set on a wire rack while you prepare the batter.

NEW YORK STYLE CHEESECAKE

CHEESECAKE BATTER

Follow the CHEESECAKE mixing directions on page 93.

- [ ] 3 packages CREAM CHEESE
  (8 oz packages, regular cream cheese)
- [ ] 2 TBSP CORN STARCH
- [ ] 1 1/2 cups SUGAR
- [ ] 1 1/2 tsp VANILLA
- [ ] 3 EGGS
- [ ] 1/2 cup HEAVY CREAM

Pour on top of baked SPONGE CAKE CRUST.

BAKING DIRECTIONS

Bake 1 hour and 15 minutes at 350° or till edges are brown and top golden. Follow baking directions given on page 93, namely, once baked, remove from water bath pan. Put on wire rack for two hours. When room temperature, refrigerate for at least four hours Overnight is best. Sprinkle with POWDERED SUGAR before serving, or serve with RASPBERRY SAUCE.

RASPBERRY SAUCE

Mix the SYRUP MIXTURE together in a small saucepan.

SYRUP MIXTURE

- [ ] 1 cup WATER
- [ ] 1/8 tsp SALT
- [ ] 2 TBSP CORN STARCH
- [ ] 2/3 cup sugar

Cook the SYRUP MIXTURE over medium heat until it comes to a rolling boil. Add the raspberries and cook a few minutes until it returns to a boil and the syrup is fruit colored.

- [ ] 2 cups RASPBERRIES (fresh or frozen)

Put in a bowl with a pouring spout, so that each person can take as much sauce as they wish on their slice of cheesecake.

MARBLE CHEESECAKE

This Marble Cheesecake has a chocolate crust. The filling is the same as the New York Style Cheesecake only with chocolate swirls.

Bring refrigerated ingredients to room temperature (page 205). Prepare an 8" springform pan (page 92). Preheat the oven to 350°.

CHOCOLATE CRUST

Melt CHOCOLATE in the micro oven (see page 209).
- ☐ 1 1/2 squares SEMI-SWEET BAKING CHOCOLATE

Sift and mix DRY INGREDIENTS.

DRY INGREDIENTS
- ☐ 1 cup G-F CAKE FLOUR   ☐ 1/4 tsp SALT
- ☐ 1/2 tsp XANTHAN GUM

SHORTENING INGREDIENTS
- ☐ 1/3 cup BUTTER   ☐ 1/4 cup SUGAR
- ☐ 1 EGG YOLK   ☐ 1/2 tsp VANILLA

Beat SHORTENING INGREDIENTS together with an electric mixer. Stir the MELTED CHOCOLATE into the SHORTENING INGREDIENTS, then add the DRY INGREDIENTS.

Pat dough into the bottom (not the sides) of the pan.
Bake at 350° for 15 to 18 minutes or till lightly brown.

CHEESECAKE BATTER
Use the recipe on page 95 to make a Cheesecake batter.

CHOCOLATE BATTER
Melt CHOCOLATE in micro safe mixing bowl (page 209).
- ☐ 2 squares SEMI-SWEET BAKING CHOCOLATE

Pour 1 1/4 cups of the CHEESECAKE BATTER into the melted CHOCOLATE. Stir till blended.

MARBLE CHEESECAKE

You now have a CHEESECAKE BATTER, a CHOCOLATE BATTER and a baked crust.

Pour half of the VANILLA BATTER over the baked crust.

Spoon half of the CHOCOLATE BATTER on top of the VANILLA batter making 5 dollops:

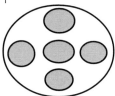

Pour the remaining VANILLA BATTER over the dollops

Spoon the remaining CHOCOLATE BATTER over the VANILLA BATTER. Try not to put the new dollops over the prior dollops.

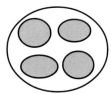

Use a butter knife to cut through the batter (not the crust) making three concentric circles. Hold the knife at an angle as you cut and swirl.

BAKING DIRECTIONS

Bake 1 hour and 15 minutes at 350° or till the top is golden brown and the middle set. Follow the directions given on page 93, namely, once baked, gently remove from water bath pan. Put on wire rack and do not disturb it for two hours; then refrigerate for at least four hours. Overnight is best.

FRENCH CHEESECAKE

The New York Style Cheesecake has a smooth top. No sinking in the middle after baking. The French Cheesecake is frosted with whipped cream and topped with fresh strawberries. It is better to have the French Cheesecake sink in the middle to create a cradle for the berries, so this cake is baked without the foil and without the water bath.

Bring refrigerated ingredients to room temperature (page 205).
Preheat oven to 350⁰.
Butter the bottom and sides of an 8" springform pan.

PASTRY CRUST

Sift and mix DRY INGREDIENTS.
DRY INGREDIENTS
- ☐ 1 cup G-F CAKE FLOUR
- ☐ 1/2 tsp XANTHAN GUM
- ☐ 1/4 tsp SALT

Beat BUTTER and SUGAR with an electric mixer till creamy.
BUTTER MIXTURE
- ☐ 1/3 cup BUTTER (room temperature)
- ☐ 1/4 cup SUGAR

Add EGG YOLK and VANILLA to BUTTER MIXTURE.
- ☐ 1 EGG YOLK
- ☐ 1 tsp VANILLA

Mix in DRY INGREDIENTS. Work the dough with your hands till it forms a ball. Press the dough into the 8" springform pan.
Prick the dough 5 or 6 times to avoid puffing while baking.

BAKING DIRECTIONS

Bake the crust 15 minutes or till slightly golden.
Remove from oven and set on a wire rack while you prepare the batter.

FRENCH CHEESECAKE

Beat the CHEESE INGREDIENTS with an electric mixer paddle on medium speed. Add the ingredients in the order given. Beat a few minutes until batter is smooth and creamy.

CHEESE INGREDIENTS
- ☐ 2 (8 oz) packages CREAM CHEESE (regular not low fat)
- ☐ 3/4 cup SUGAR
- ☐ 2 EGGS + 1 EGG WHITE
- ☐ 1/4 cup HEAVY CREAM
- ☐ 1/4 cup SOUR CREAM
- ☐ 1/2 tsp VANILLA

BAKING DIRECTIONS

Pour the beaten CHEESE INGREDIENTS into the baked pastry crust. Bake at 300^0 for one hour or till edges are set and center barely giggles. Cool the cake in the spring form pan. It will pull away from the sides and deflate forming a ridge on the top of the cake. Refrigerate the cake in the springform pan overnight.

STRAWBERRY TOPPING

Wash and remove stems from STRAWBERRIES.
- ☐ 1 Pint STRAWBERRIES

Cut the STRAWBERRIES into one inch slices. Place them in a bowl and sprinkle with the following:
- ☐ 2 TBSP LEMON JUICE   ☐ 1/2 cup of SUGAR

Set aside while you make the WHIPPED CREAM.

WHIPPED CREAM FROSTING

Make WHIPPED CREAM using the recipe on page 210.

Remove the CHEESECAKE from the springform pan and transfer it to a serving plate lined with wax paper. Drain the berries and reserve the juice to pour over the cake when serving. Place the strawberries inside the cake ridge. Frost the cake with WHIPPED CREAM, remove the wax paper and serve.

RICOTTA CHEESECAKE

This Cheesecake is the easiest to bake. It has no separate crust, no foil wrap, no water bath. It can be served at room temperature or cold from the refrigerator.

Using the paddle attachment to an electric mixer. Beat the RICOTTA until it is creamy (about 10 minutes).
- ☐ 3 cups RICOTTA (whole milk)

Meanwhile, preheat oven to 350°.
Butter and flour 10" tart pan (page 206).
- ☐ 2 TBSP BUTTER
- ☐ 2 TBSP RICE FLOUR

Combine FRUIT MIXTURE and set aside.
FRUIT MIXTURE
- ☐ 2 tsp ORANGE RIND
- ☐ 1 tsp LEMON RIND
- ☐ 1 TBSP chopped CITRON (optional)

Once the RICOTTA is creamy, put the electric mixer on medium speed and gradually add the following ingredients in the order given:
- ☐ 2 TBSP CORN STARCH
- ☐ 1/2 tsp SALT
- ☐ 3 EGGS (one at a time)
- ☐ 1 cup SUGAR

Stir the FRUIT MIXTURE into the batter.

BAKING DIRECTIONS
Bake 350° for 50 minutes or until golden brown and set in the middle. Let cool in the baking pan till room temperature.

Sprinkle with POWDERED SUGAR and serve at room temperature or refrigerate and serve cold.

Muffins & Buns

Corn Muffins 103

Blueberry Muffins 104

Raisin Bran 105

Zucchini Muffins 106

Orange-Cranberry Scones 107

Crumb Buns 109

Cinnamon Buns 110

Sticky Buns   111

Hot Cross Buns 112

MUFFINS

CUPCAKES, MUFFINS AND BUNS

A cupcake is an individual sized cake. It is usually frosted and served as a dessert. Most any cake recipe can be used to make cupcakes. The muffin is an individual sized sweet bread — not as sweet as a cupcake. Buns also are sweetbreads only with yeast as their primary leavening agent.

HOW TO BAKE MUFFINS

1. Bring refrigerated ingredients to room temperature.
Spray the muffin pan or put a paper liner in each cup. The given muffin recipes fill a regular size 12 cup muffin pan or a large, coffee shop size, 6 cup muffin pan.

2. Preheat oven to the temperature given in the **BAKING DIRECTIONS.**

3. Sift **DRY INGREDIENTS** into a bowl. Mix with a large spoon.

4. Measure **LIQUID INGREDIENTS** into another bowl.

5. Measure **SHORTENING INGREDIENTS** into an electric mixing bowl and beat until light and fluffy. Add **EGGS** one at a time, beating well after each addition.

6. Alternate **DRY** and **LIQUID INGREDIENTS** into **SHORTENING** (page 57). Do not over beat the batter.

7. If the recipe calls for **ADDITIONAL INGREDIENTS,** fold them into the batter.

8. Divide the batter evenly into the baking cups.
Bake according to the given **BAKING DIRECTIONS.**

CORN MUFFINS

The corn muffin is a versatile muffin. It can be made plain and served in place of bread at dinner, or add raisins and eat it as a snack.

Follow the MUFFIN BAKING directions on the last page.

DRY INGREDIENTS

- ☐ 1/2 cup CORN MEAL (fine)
- ☐ 1 cup MASAREPA (precooked corn meal)
- ☐ 1/2 cup G-F ALL PURPOSE FLOUR
- ☐ 1 tsp SALT
- ☐ 1 1/2 tsp BAKING POWDER
- ☐ 1/2 tsp BAKING SODA

LIQUID INGREDIENTS

- ☐ 3/4 cup BUTTERMILK
- ☐ 1 tsp ORANGE RIND

SHORTENING INGREDIENTS

- ☐ 1/3 cup LIGHT OLIVE OIL
- ☐ 1/2 cup SUGAR

EGGS ☐ 3 EGGS

ADDITIONAL INGREDIENTS (optional)
FRUITS ☐ 1 cup GOLDEN RAISINS

BAKING DIRECTIONS
Bake at 400° FOR 15 to 20 MINUTES or till golden brown.

BLUEBERRY MUFFINS

You can make this recipe with fresh blueberries (rinsed and dried with a paper towel) or frozen blueberries straight from the freezer. We made six large blueberry muffins, but this recipe works just as well with a 12 muffin pan.

Follow the MUFFIN BAKING directions on page 102.

DRY INGREDIENTS

- ☐ 2 cups G-F CAKE FLOUR
- ☐ 2 tsp BAKING POWDER
- ☐ 1 1/2 tsp XANTHAN GUM
- ☐ 3/4 tsp SALT
- ☐ 1 tsp BAKING SODA
- ☐ 1 TBSP EGG REPLACER

LIQUID INGREDIENTS

- ☐ 2/3 cup BUTTERMILK
- ☐ 1 tsp ORANGE RIND

SHORTENING INGREDIENTS

- ☐ 4 TBSP BUTTER
- ☐ 1 cup SUGAR

EGGS ☐ 2 EGGS + 2 EGG WHITES

ADDITIONAL INGREDIENTS

BLUEBERRIES ☐ 1 1/2 cup BLUEBERRIES

Spoon the batter into the muffin tin.
Sprinkle the top of each muffin with SUGAR.

SUGAR ☐ 2 TBSP SUGAR

BAKING DIRECTIONS

Bake at 375⁰ FOR 15 to 20 MINUTES or till golden brown and toothpick comes out when inserted into the middle of a muffin.

RAISIN BRAN MUFFINS

Mom baked raisin bran muffins using the recipe from the side of a box of Kellogg's All-Bran Cereal. She would always tell me how healthy they were. Health was of no interest to me. I ate the muffins because they tasted good.

It takes a lot of ingredients to make a rice bran muffin taste like Mom's All-Bran Muffin. Still, for that moment of nostalgia, it's worth the effort.

Follow the MUFFIN BAKING directions on page 102.

DRY INGREDIENTS
- [ ] 1/4 cup BROWN RICE FLOUR
- [ ] 1/4 cup TAPIOCA STARCH
- [ ] 1/3 cup QUINOA FLAKES
- [ ] 1/4 cup WHOLE GRAIN TEFF
- [ ] 2 tsp BAKING POWDER
- [ ] 1 1/2 tsp XANTHAN GUM
- [ ] 1/2 cup RICE BRAN
- [ ] 1/4 cup ALMOND MEAL
- [ ] 1 TBSP BUCKWHEAT
- [ ] 1 tsp SALT
- [ ] 1 tsp BAKING SODA

LIQUID INGREDIENTS
- [ ] 1/3 cup MILK
- [ ] 1 tsp VANILLA

SHORTENING INGREDIENTS
- [ ] 1/2 cup LIGHT OLIVE OIL
- [ ] 3/4 cup SUGAR

EGGS
- [ ] 2 EGGS

ADDITIONAL INGREDIENTS
- [ ] 2/3 cup RAISINS

BAKING DIRECTIONS
Bake at 375° FOR 18 to 20 MINUTES or till golden brown and a toothpick comes out clean when inserted in the center of the muffin.

ZUCCHINI MUFFINS

The Zucchini Muffin was another one of those "healthy" desserts many of us enjoyed growing up. Zucchini holds moisture in the muffin without giving it a vegetable taste, so this tasty muffin remains popular today.

PREPARE ZUCCHINI
Wash 3 small or 2 medium sized ZUCCHINI. Cut off the tips. Grate the zucchini (skins and all). Squeeze out the moisture with a strainer and paper towels, then measure a packed cup of grated zucchini.

Sift and mix DRY INGREDIENTS.
DRY INGREDIENTS
- ☐ 1 cup G-F ALL PURPOSE FLOUR
- ☐ 1 1/2 tsp BAKING POWDER
- ☐ 1/2 tsp BAKING SODA
- ☐ 1/2 tsp XANTHAN GUM
- ☐ 3/4 tsp SALT
- ☐ 1 tsp CINNAMON
- ☐ 1/4 tsp NUTMEG

Beat SHORTENING INGREDIENTS with an electric mixer.
SHORTENING INGREDIENTS
- ☐ 1/4 cup BUTTER (or MARGARINE)
- ☐ 1/2 cup SUGAR

Beat in EGGS, then stir in the ZUCCHINI.
- ☐ 2 EGGS
- ☐ 1 cup ZUCCHINI

Fold in RAISINS and WALNUTS
- ☐ 1/2 cup RAISINS
- ☐ 1/2 cup WALNUTS (chopped)

BAKING DIRECTIONS
Bake at 400° FOR 15 to 20 MINUTES or till golden brown and toothpick comes out clean.

ORANGE-CRANBERRY SCONE

Like the muffin, the scone is not too sweet and goes well with a hot beverage. The scone looks harder to make than it is. It is mixed much like pie crust dough, patted into an 8" circle, then cut it into 8 triangles.

Put CRISCO in the freezer for an hour before baking. Preheat oven to 375°. Spray a cookie sheet. Sift and mx DRY INGREDIENTS.

DRY INGREDIENTS

- ☐ 2 cups G-F CAKE FLOUR
- ☐ 1 1/2 tsp XANTHAN GUM
- ☐ 4 tsp BAKING POWDER
- ☐ 1 TBSP EGG REPLACER
- ☐ 1/2 cup SUGAR
- ☐ 1/2 tsp SALT
- ☐ 1 tsp BAKING SODA

Cut SHORTENING into DRY INGREDIENTS (page 208).

SHORTENING

- ☐ 1/4 cup COLD BUTTER
- ☐ 1/4 cup COLD CRISCO

Beat LIQUID INGREDIENTS together with a fork, then add to the batter and mix into a soft dough.

LIQUID INGREDIENTS

- ☐ 1/4 cup BUTTERMILK
- ☐ 1 EGG
- ☐ 1 tsp ORANGE RIND

Fold the CRANBERRIES into the dough.

- ☐ 1/2 cup DRIED CRANBERRIES

Put the dough on a silicone sheet dusted with RICE FLOUR. Pat the dough into a pie shape 8" in diameter and an inch thick. Cut the dough into 8 triangles (see picture page 101). Place the scones on a sprayed cookie sheet. Brush tops with EVAPORATED MILK. Sprinkle with SUGAR.

- ☐ 1 TBSP EVAPORATED MILK
- ☐ 1 TBSP SUGAR

BAKING DIRECTIONS

Bake at 375° for 15 - 18 minutes or till golden brown.

HOW TO BAKE RAISED BUNS

Crumb Buns, Cinnamon Buns, Sticky Buns, Cross Buns are raised buns. They all start with the same raised batter:

1. Bring EGGS, BUTTER and BUTTERMILK to room temperature (page 205).

2. Mix WATER and SUGAR into a small bowl. Sprinkle YEAST on top and set aside a few minutes till bubbly.

YEAST INGREDIENTS
- ☐ 1/4 LUKE WARM WATER
- ☐ 1 TBSP YEAST   ☐ 1 tsp SUGAR

3. Sift and mix DRY INGREDIENTS in an electric mixer bowl.

DRY INGREDIENTS
- ☐ 2 cups G-F CAKE FLOUR   ☐ 1 tsp SALT
- ☐ 1 1/2 tsp XANTHAN GUM   ☐ 1/3 cup SUGAR
- ☐ 1 tsp BAKING POWDER   ☐ 1 tsp GELATIN
- ☐ 2 tsp EGG REPLACER

4. Mix LIQUID INGREDIENTS till blended

LIQUID INGREDIENTS
- ☐ 1 EGG + 2 EGG WHITES (beaten together)
- ☐ 1/2 cup BUTTERMILK
- ☐ 3 TBSP BUTTER (melted)   ☐ 1 tsp VANILLA

5. Add LIQUID INGREDIENTS and YEAST MIXTURE to the DRY INGREDIENTS. Mix with a large spoon till blended. Beat with an electric mixer dough hook for 5 minutes or till smooth.

6. Keep the dough in a warm place for 1 to 1 1/2 hours until double in bulk. To create a warm place, set the oven on 300° for 15 SECONDS. Turn the oven off and place the baking pan in the center of the oven. Leave the oven light on. Once double in bulk, remove the pan from the oven and preheat the oven to the temperature given in the **BAKING DIRECTIONS**.

CRUMB BUNS

Growing up in New York, it was a Sunday treat to walk to the corner bakery and buy oven fresh crumb buns. These gluten free Crumb Buns taste even better than I remember.

BUTTER a square (8" X 8" X 2") glass cake pan.
☐ 1 TBSP BUTTER

Make a RAISED BUN batter (steps 1 to 5, page 108). Pour BATTER into cake pan and allow to rise till double in bulk (step 6).

Once the dough has risen, preheat oven to 350° and make the CRUMB TOPPING.

CRUMB TOPPING

Sift and mix DRY INGREDIENTS.

DRY INGREDIENTS
☐ 1 cup G-F ALL PURPOSE FLOUR   ☐ 1/4 tsp SALT
☐ 1/2 tsp CINNAMON   ☐ 1/4 cup SUGAR
☐ 1/4 cup BROWN SUGAR   ☐ 1/4 tsp NUTMEG

Cut BUTTER into DRY INGREDIENTS (page 208).
☐ 5 TBSP BUTTER

Use your fingers to work the mixture into 1" crumbs.

Melt BUTTER and brush on the risen dough.
☐ 2 tsp BUTTER

Cover buttered dough with the **CRUMB TOPPING**.
Cut the dough to form 9 square buns (3 rows, 3 buns per row).

BAKING DIRECTIONS

Bake at 350° for 30 minutes or till brown around the edge and pulls away from sides of the pan. Sprinkle liberally with POWDERED SUGAR and serve.
☐ 1/4 cup POWDERED SUGAR

CINNAMON BUNS

To make a Cinnamon Bun, the raised bun batter needs to be patted into a square, fill with nuts and raisins, then rolled and cut into slices. You will need a silicone mat (the same used for pie crusts), a sharp knife to cut the dough and a spatula to help roll the dough.

BUTTER a square (8" X 8" X 2"), glass, cake pan.

☐ 1 TBSP BUTTER

Mix the BUN FILLING and set aside.

BUN FILLING

☐ 1/2 cup BROWN SUGAR   ☐ 1/3 cup RAISINS
☐ 1/3 cup CHOPPED WALNUTS ☐ 1 tsp CINNAMON

Make a RAISED BUN batter (steps 1 to 5, page 108).
Liberally sprinkle a silicone mat with RICE FLOUR. Put the dough in the middle of the floured mat. The dough will be sticky, so sprinkle the dough and your hands with RICE FLOUR. Pat the dough into a rectangle 8" X 12". Brush the dough with melted BUTTER

☐ 2 tsp MELTED BUTTER

Spread the BUN FILLING over the melted BUTTER. Roll the dough, jelly roll style, into a roll 12" long. If it sticks to the mat, use more RICE FLOUR and a spatula to help roll it over. Cut the dough into 9 buns. Place the buns into the square pan (3 rows, 3 buns per row) filling side up, dough sides touching. Let the buns rise till double in bulk (step 6, page 108).

BAKING DIRECTIONS

Preheat oven to 350°. Bake for 30 minutes or till golden brown. Cool to room temperature in the cake pan, then cover the buns with a GLAZE and serve.

GLAZE

Beat the following ingredients till smooth.

☐ 1 cup SIFTED POWDERED SUGAR
☐ 2 TBSP WARM WATER

Favorite Desserts Made Gluten Free

STICKY BUNS

Sticky Buns are baked individually in a cupcake pan. You can use a 12 cup pan, or make 6 large sticky bums with a 6 cup pan, as we did.

Butter the cupcake pan. ☐ 1 TBSP BUTTER
Place 5 PECAN HALVES, rounded side down, in each cup (3 PECAN HALVES per cup for a 12 cup pan).
☐ 30 PECAN HALVES (36 for a 12 cup pan)

MIX CINNAMON and SUGAR till blended.
☐ 1/3 cup BROWN SUGAR ☐ 1 tsp CINNAMON
Divide the CINNAMON SUGAR evenly among the cups.
Top with a 1/2 tsp BUTTER per cup (1/4 tsp for a 12 cup pan).

Mix the BUN FILLING and set aside.
BUN FILLING
☐ 1/2 cup LIGHT BROWN SUGAR
☐ 1 tsp CINNAMON ☐ 1/2 cup CHOPPED PECANS

Make a RAISED BUN batter (steps 1 to 5, page 108). Sprinkle a silicone mat with RICE FLOUR. Place the RAISED BUN batter in the middle of the mat. Liberally powder the sticky dough (and your hands) with RICE FLOUR. Pat the dough into a 8" X 12" rectangle. Brush the dough with MELTED BUTTER.
☐ 2 tsp BUTTER
Spread the BUN FILLING over the melted BUTTER. Roll the dough jelly roll style into a 12" long roll. If it sticks to the mat, use more RICE FLOUR and a spatula to help roll it over. Cut the dough into 6 buns (or 12 buns for a 12 cupcake pan).
Place the buns into the baking pan cut side up.
Let rise til double in bulk (step 6, page 108).

BAKING DIRECTIONS
Preheat oven to 350⁰. Bake for 20 minutes or till golden brown.

HOT CROSS BUNS

Hot Cross Buns were a seasonal treat. Mom said you could give up desserts for Lent and still eat a Hot Cross Bun. It didn't count as a dessert. I didn't know why. They tasted as good to me as any other bun.

BUTTER a square (8" X 8" X 2") glass cake pan.

☐ 1 TBSP BUTTER

Make a RAISED BUN batter (steps 1 to 5, page 108). Once the batter is mixed, fold in the FRUIT.

FRUIT   ☐ 1/3 cup of RAISINS and/or CITRON**

**Use all RAISINS or all CITRON or a combination of both.

Make 9 buns by using a large serving spoon to drop the dough into the baking pan making 3 rows with 3 buns per row. Let dough rise for an hour or till double in bulk (step 6, page 108).

Preheat oven to 350°. Brush bun tops with EGG SUBSTITUTE.

☐ 2 tsp EGG SUBSTITUTE

BAKING DIRECTIONS

Bake at 350° for 30 minutes or till golden brown. Once the buns are room temperature give each its distinctive white cross icing.

WHITE ICING

Use a tube of store-bought WHITE ICING to make a horizontal line on each bun. Then cross it in the middle with a vertical line.

- or -

Make WHITE ICING by mixing SUGAR and WATER till smooth

☐ 3/4 cup POWDERED SUGAR

☐ 2 tsp WARM WATER

Cut a very small hole in the corner of a plastic sandwich bag. Pour the icing into the bag and squeeze gently to decorate the bun. If you have extra icing, go over each cross a second time, making it wider and higher.

Pie Index

HOW TO MAKE PIE CRUST

Making a flaky, gluten free pie crust is easy with the right tools (pastry blender, silicone mat, rolling pin, wax paper). Temperature is important. Shortening and water must be ice cold.

1. An hour before starting:
Put the **SHORTENING** into the freezer and the **WATER** into the refrigerator.

2. Mix **LIQUID INGREDIENTS** in a small bowl till blended.

3. Sift and mix **DRY INGREDIENTS**.

4. Cut **SHORTENING** into **DRY INGREDIENTS**.
You can use two knives going in opposite directions, or a manual pastry blender or a food processor (see page 208). The object is to incorporate the shortening into the flour until it looks coarse or pea shaped.

5. Add **LIQUID INGREDIENTS**.
Work the dough with your hands until it is crumbly. Add LIQUID INGREDIENTS to form a smooth ball. If the dough is crumbly, add another tablespoon of ICE WATER. If the dough is sticky, you added too much water. Don't add any more flour, just dust with RICE FLOUR to make it easy to handle.

6. Roll the dough.
Place the dough onto a silicone mat lightly floured with rice flour. Sprinkle the top of the dough with rice flour. Pat the dough into a circle. Place a sheet of wax paper over the dough. Roll the dough to the required size starting from the center and working outward until the dough is 1" greater than the rim of the pie pan. Remove the wax paper.

HOW TO MAKE PIE CRUST

7.   Place the dough into the pie pan.

Placing the dough into the pie pan can be a challenge if it isn't lined up properly. To center the dough, place the pie pan upside-down in the middle of the rolled dough. Put your hand under the middle of the silicone sheet. Flip pie pan, dough and silicone sheet all in one movement. Remove the silicone sheet. The dough should fit neatly into the pie pan with about an inch of dough hanging over the sides. Do not stretch or pull the dough or it will shrink when baked.

FINISHING THE EDGE OF A SINGLE PIE CRUST
FINISH EDGE WITH A FORK

Tuck the extra inch of dough under the rim.
Use a fork to press the dough down.

FLUTE THE EDGE

Pressing with a fork looks good, but fluting makes a pie look like it was made by a "pro." And it's not hard to do. Tuck the extra inch of dough under the rim, then pinch the rim dough into little grooves using your thumb and index finger to sculpt the dough. See picture of the fluted edge of the Pecan Pie on page 133.

FINISHING THE EDGE OF A DOUBLE PIE CRUST

Tuck the extending inch under the bottom rim of crust, making a thick rim of dough. You can flute the edge or finish it with a fork. Finishing the edge of the crust with a fork is best for fruit pies, because it seals the crust and holds in the juices. See picture of Blueberry Pie on page 121.

BAKING THE PIE

Follow the **BAKING DIRECTIONS** given in the recipe. If you are baking a fruit pie, place an aluminium lined cookie sheet on the oven rack beneath the pies to catch any fruit juice that might bubble over.

SINGLE PIE CRUST

Follow PIE CRUST directions on pages 114 and 115.

SHORTENING
- ☐ 7 TBSP CRISCO (cold from freezer).

LIQUID INGREDIENTS
- ☐ 1 1/2 tsp WHITE VINEGAR
- ☐ 1 1/2 tsp EGG SUBSTITUTE
- ☐ 2 TBSP ICE WATER

DRY INGREDIENTS
- ☐ 1 1/2 cups G-F ALL PURPOSE FLOUR
- ☐ 3/4 tsp SALT   ☐ 1 1/2 tsp SUGAR
- ☐ 1 tsp XANTHAN GUM

ADDITIONAL WATER
- ☐ up to 3 TBSP WATER

BAKED SINGLE PIE CRUST

Place the dough into a pie pan. Finish the edges with a fork, or flute the edge using the directions on page 115. To prevent puffing while baking, prick the bottom with a fork a dozen times, evenly spaced. Brush the pie crust with EGG SUBSTITUTE.

- ☐ 1 TBSP EGG SUBSTITUTE

Bake in a preheated at 450° for 10 to 12 minutes or till golden brown around the edge.

UNBAKED SINGLE PIE CRUST

Line the pie pan with the dough. Flute the edges, but do not prick the dough with a fork. Follow the baking directions given in the recipe.

Favorite Desserts Made Gluten Free

DOUBLE PIE CRUST

Follow PIE CRUST directions on pages 114 and 115.

SHORTENING
- ☐ 3/4 cup CRISCO (cold from freezer)

LIQUID INGREDIENTS
- ☐ 1 TBSP WHITE VINEGAR
- ☐ 1 TBSP EGG SUBSTITUTE ☐ 2 TBSP ICE WATER

DRY INGREDIENTS
- ☐ 2 1/2 cups G-F ALL PURPOSE FLOUR
- ☐ 2 tsp XANTHAN GUM
- ☐ 1 TBSP SUGAR ☐ 1 tsp SALT

ADDITIONAL WATER
- ☐ UP TO 1/4 cup ICE WATER

BOTTOM CRUST
Roll the bottom crust and place it in the pan. Trim the edge so that the edge of the pie crust is flush with the pie pan edge.

TOP CRUST
Roll out the remaining dough on a silicone sheet to an inch greater than the rim of the pie pan. Once the pie is filled, flip the silicone sheet over the pie filling. Fold the edge of the top crust under the bottom crust. Finish the edge of the crust using the directions for a double crust on page 115.

BRUSH AND SPRINKLE TOP PIE CRUST
Brush the top pie with EGG SUBSTITUTE or EVAPORATED MILK..
- ☐ 1 TBSP EGG SUBSTITUTE (or EVAPORATED MILK)

Sprinkle the top with sugar.
- ☐ 1 TBSP SUGAR.

Bake the pie using the directions given in the recipe.

THE LATTICE CRUST

Roll out the remaining (top crust) dough to the size of the pie pan. Use a pastry wheel to cut the dough into decorative 1" strips. Assemble the lattice crust on a silicone sheet, and then flip it over onto the filled pie.

Place the largest strip in the middle, the second largest next to it and third largest at the end:

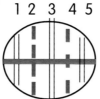

Take the largest remaining strip and weave it horizontally by lifting strips 2 and 4.

Lattice the next two strips by lifting strips 1, 3 and 5.

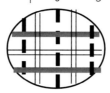

WINGING IT

If, like me, you are technically challenged, place the horizontal stripes over the vertical strips without weaving. It will make a **RFT** (Reasonable Facsimile Thereof). See Black Cherry Pie page 121.

FINISHING TOUCHES

The bottom crust should extend over the pie pan by an inch. Fold bottom inch of dough over the rim of the top crust. Flute the edge or press the dough with a fork. Brush with EVAPORATED MILK or EGG WHITE. Sprinkle with SUGAR.

"GRAHAM" CRUST

You could bake "Graham" Crackers using the recipe on page 38, and then crumble them up to make this pie crust. But why work so hard when you can make the crust with cereal crumbs?

Make CEREAL CRUMBS using directions on page 210.
Preheat oven to 350°. Butter a 9" pie pan.

☐ 1 TBSP BUTTER

Use a spoon to mix the CEREAL INGREDIENTS in a bowl.

CEREAL INGREDIENTS

☐ 2 cups CEREAL CRUMBS	☐ 1/4 tsp CINNAMON
☐ 1 TBSP CORN STARCH	☐ 1 TBSP HONEY

Add BUTTER to CEREAL INGREDIENTS. Use your hands to mix till blended.

☐ 1/3 cup BUTTER or MARGARINE (room temperature).

Pour the crumbs into a pie pan. Use the back of a measuring cup to press the crumbs evenly on the bottom of the pan. Use the back of a spoon to press the crumbs around the sides of the pan.

BAKING DIRECTIONS

Bake at 350° for 7 minutes until crust is just set.

CHOCOLATE CRUMB CRUST

The CHOCOLATE CRUMB CRUST is made the same as the above "GRAHAM" CRUST only substituting the following for the CEREAL INGREDIENTS.

CEREAL INGREDIENTS

☐ 1 3/4 cups CEREAL CRUMBS
☐ 2 TBSP BAKING COCOA
☐ 1/4 cup SUGAR

ALMOND CRUMB CRUST

Follow the "GRAHAM" CRUST directions on the last page substituting the following for the CEREAL INGREDIENTS.

CEREAL INGREDIENTS
- ☐ 1 2/3 cups CEREAL CRUMBS
- ☐ 1/2 cup ALMOND MEAL
- ☐ 1/2 tsp ALMOND EXTRACT
- ☐ 1 TBSP CORN STARCH
- ☐ 2 TBSP SUGAR

NUT CRUMB CRUST

Make CEREAL CRUMBS using directions on page 210.
Preheat oven to 350⁰. Butter a 9" pie pan.

☐ 1 TBSP BUTTER

Chop Macadamia or Cashew Nut or Walnuts or any combination of these nuts into small pieces.

☐ 1/2 cup CHOPPED NUTS

Mix the NUTS with CEREAL INGREDIENTS in a bowl:
CEREAL INGREDIENTS
- ☐ 1 2/3 cups CEREAL CRUMBS
- ☐ 1 TBSP CORN STARCH
- ☐ 2 TBSP SUGAR

Add BUTTER. Use your hands to mix till blended.

☐ 1/3 cup BUTTER or MARGARINE (room temperature)

Pour the crumbs into a pie pan. Use the back of a measuring cup to press the crumbs evenly on the bottom of the pan. Use the back of a spoon to press the crumbs around the sides of the pan.

BAKING DIRECTIONS
Bake at 350⁰ for 7 minutes until crust is just set.

Fruit Pie

Black Cherry   122

Pineapple Cheese   123

Deep Dish Apple   124

Fresh Peach   126

Blueberry   128

Strawberry-Rhubarb 129

Lemon Meringue   130

Key Lime Pie   132

BLACK CHERRY PIE

You could bake a fresh cherry pie, but why bother unless you own the tree and the fruit is free? The problem is pits. Using a manual cherry pit remover is tedious and time consuming. It might make sense if fresh cherries were your only option. Not today. There are canned and frozen cherries. Frozen cherries are closest to fresh. They make a great cherry pie and that is what we used in this recipe.

CHERRY INGREDIENTS

- ☐ 4 cups frozen BING (DARK SWEET) CHERRIES (two 12 oz packages of frozen CHERRIES)
- ☐ 3 TBSP MINUTE TAPIOCA
- ☐ 1 TBSP LEMON JUICE
- ☐ 1 cup SUGAR

Mix the CHERRY INGREDIENTS in a large bowl and let stand at room temperature for 45 minutes. Stir before placing in the pie shell.

Preheat the oven to 400°.
Make a lattice crust using the directions on page 118.
Put the CHERRY FILING into the pie shell and dot with BUTTER.

- ☐ 1 TBSP BUTTER

Put the top crust in place. Brush with EGG SUBSTITUTE or EVAPORATED MILK. Sprinkle SUGAR on top.

- ☐ 2 tsp EGG SUBSTITUTE (or EVAPORATED MILK)
- ☐ 2 tsp SUGAR

BAKING DIRECTIONS

Bake at 400° for 15 minutes, then cover with a silicone or metal edge protector. Reduce heat to 350° and bake another 30 minutes until the crust is golden brown and the filling bubbly.

PINEAPPLE CHEESE PIE

This was a favorite treat in New York before there were supermarkets. Large pies were made at a local bakery, delivered to the neighborhood grocery stores and then sold to customers by the slice.

Bring refrigerated ingredients to room temperature (page 205). Make a SINGLE PIE CRUST using the recipe on page 116. Do not prick the crust. Bake it for 7 minutes at 400°. Remove from oven and set aside.

PINEAPPLE FILLING

Put following ingredients in a small saucepan over a medium heat.

- ☐ 2 cups CRUSHED PINEAPPLE (including juice) (two 8 oz cans of CRUSHED PINEAPPLE)
- ☐ 2 1/2 TBSP CORN STARCH
- ☐ 1/4 tsp SALT ☐ 1/3 cup SUGAR

Stir till it comes to a boil. Remove from heat and set aside.

CHEESE TOPPING

Beat the following together for 5 minutes.

- ☐ 2 EGGS
- ☐ 3/4 cup SUGAR ☐ 1/2 tsp VANILLA
- ☐ 8 oz CREAM CHEESE**
- ☐ 1/4 cup SOUR CREAM**

** Regular is best. Reduced fat can be used, but not fat free.

Spread the **PINEAPPLE FILLING** over the baked pie crust. Gently pour the **CHEESE TOPPING** over the PINEAPPLE FILLING.

BAKING DIRECTIONS

Bake at 350° for 45 minutes or till just set, i.e., with a slight jiggle in the middle. Cool to room temperature, then refrigerate several hours. Sprinkle top with POWDERED SUGAR and serve.

DEEP DISH APPLE PIE

Whoever said "easy as apple pie" never baked one. The problem is that apples vary in sweetness and texture. Granny Smith apples are the most popular for baking. Golden Delicious, Fuji, Jonagold, and Rome Beauty apples work as well. This is the time to experiment until you find the apple you like best. As for texture, it is important to have uniformly thin slices to avoid under-baked thick slices. The answer is the food processor. It slices apples perfectly and in seconds.

Make a single pie crust using the directions on page 114 with the following ingredients.

Make a single pie crust using the directions on page 114

PIE CRUST INGREDIENTS

SHORTENING
- ☐ 7 TBSP CRISCO *(cold from freezer)*.

LIQUID INGREDIENTS
- ☐ 1 1/2 tsp WHITE VINEGAR
- ☐ 1 1/2 tsp EGG SUBSTITUTE
- ☐ 2 TBSP ICE WATER

DRY INGREDIENTS
- ☐ 1 1/2 cups G-F ALL PURPOSE FLOUR
- ☐ 3/4 tsp SALT   ☐ 1 1/2 tsp SUGAR
- ☐ 1 tsp XANTHAN GUM

ADDITIONAL WATER
- ☐ UP TO 1/4 cup ICE WATER

PREPARE THE APPLES

Squeeze the juice from an ORANGE and put in a large bowl.
- ☐ 1/4 cup ORANGE JUICE

Wash and peel 5 or 6 apples. Use a food processor to cut the apples into very thin slices.
- ☐ 5 cups APPLES

Mix APPLES and ORANGE JUICE together.

DEEP DISH APPLE PIE

Preheat oven to 350⁰. Butter the bottom of a 9" pie pan.

☐ 1 TBSP BUTTER

Mix the FILLING INGREDIENTS in a bowl.

FILLING INGREDIENTS

☐ 1/2 cup LIGHT BROWN SUGAR

☐ 1/2 cup SUGAR

☐ 1/4 cup CORN STARCH

☐ 1/8 tsp SALT

☐ 1 tsp CINNAMON

☐ 1/4 tsp NUTMEG

Pour FILLING INGREDIENTS over the APPLES and mix with a large spoon. Fill the pie pan with the apple mixture.

Dot with BUTTER. ☐ 1 TBSP BUTTER

Cover the APPLES with the crust. Use a fork to make a large "A" in the crust. Brush the crust with EGG SUBSTITUTE or EVAPORATED MILK.

☐ 2 tsp EGG SUBSTITUTE (or EVAPORATED MILK)

Sprinkle the crust with SUGAR.

☐ 1 TBSP SUGAR

BAKING DIRECTIONS

Bake at 350⁰ for 15 minutes, then cover with a silicone or metal edge protector. Continue baking another 40 minutes or until the crust is golden brown and the apples bubbly.

Serve warm with VANILLA ICE CREAM.

FRESH PEACH PIE

Nothing better in the summer than to take large, ripe peaches and turn them into a peach pie. It takes an extra step to remove the peach skins, but it's not hard to do and the result is worth it. If skinning peaches is not your thing, or if you long for a peach pie in the middle of winter, substitute 2 packages (4 cups) of frozen peaches.

Make a DOUBLE CRUST or a LATTICE TOP CRUST (pages 117, 118).

SHORTENING MIX
- ☐ 3/4 cup CRISCO

LIQUID INGREDIENTS
- ☐ 1 TBSP WHITE VINEGAR
- ☐ 1 TBSP EGG SUBSTITUTE
- ☐ 2 TBSP ICE WATER

DRY INGREDIENTS
- ☐ 2 1/2 cups G-F ALL PURPOSE FLOUR
- ☐ 2 tsp XANTHAN GUM
- ☐ 1 TBSP SUGAR ☐ 1 tsp SALT

ADDITIONAL WATER
- ☐ UP TO 1/4 cup ICE WATER

Line the pie pan with the bottom crust.
Set the top or latticed crust aside.

PREPARE THE PEACHES

Wash 5 large ripe peaches. Fill a saucepan with water, large enough to cover a peach. Bring water to a boil. Put a peach in the boiling water for 1 minute. Remove the peach with a slated spoon. Run the peach under cold water. The skin should peel off easily. Place the peeled peach in a bowl and repeat the process for the rest of the peaches. Cut the peaches into one inch slices.

FRESH PEACH PIE

Preheat oven to 375⁰.
Mix DRY INGREDIENTS in a bowl.

DRY INGREDIENTS

- ☐ 1/4 cup CORN STARCH
- ☐ 3/4 cup SUGAR
- ☐ 1/8 tsp SALT
- ☐ 1/2 tsp CINNAMON

Pour the DRY INGREDIENTS over the sliced peaches and mix with a large spoon.

PEACHES   ☐ 4 cups of sliced PEACHES

Pour the peach mixture into the unbaked bottom crust and dot with BUTTER.

BUTTER   ☐ 1 TBSP BUTTER

Put the top crust in place. Brush it with TOPPING.

TOPPING   ☐ 2 tsp EGG SUBSTITUTE (or EVAPORATED MILK))

Sprinkle the top crust with SUGAR.

- ☐ 1 TBSP SUGAR

BAKING DIRECTIONS
Bake at 375⁰ for 15 minutes, then cover with a silicone or metal edge protector. Continue baking for another 30 to 35 minute or until crust is golden brown and filling is bubbly.

Serve warm with VANILLA ICE CREAM.

BLUEBERRY PIE

This pie is best baked when blueberries are in season, however you can use frozen blueberries to enjoy this pie any time of the year.

Make a double pie crust using the recipe on page 117. Line the pie pan with the bottom crust. Make the top crust and set it aside. Preheat the oven to 375°.
Wash BLUEBERRIES in cold water.

☐ 4 cups (2 pints) BLUEBERRIES

Drain, pat dry and set aside in a large bowl.

Mix DRY INGREDIENTS in a bowl.

DRY INGREDIENTS

☐ 6 TBSP CORN STARCH ☐ 1/4 tsp SALT
☐ 1/2 tsp CINNAMON ☐ 1 cup SUGAR
☐ 1/2 tsp LEMON RIND

Add DRY INGREDIENTS to BLUEBERRIES and mix till blended. Pour the mixture into the unbaked bottom crust. Dot with BUTTER. ☐ 1 TBSP BUTTER

Cover BLUEBERRIES with top crust. With a fork, make a large "B" on the top crust. Brush the top crust with EGG SUBSTITUTE or EVAPORATED MILK, then sprinkle the top with SUGAR

☐ 2 tsp EGG SUBSTITUTE (or EVAPORATED MILK)
☐ 2 tsp SUGAR

BAKING DIRECTIONS

Bake at 375° for 15 minutes, then cover with a silicone or metal edge protector. Continue baking another 30 to 35 minutes or until the crust is golden brown and the filling bubbly.

STRAWBERRY RHUBARB PIE

Even those who are not rhubarb enthusiasts will love this flavorful pie. We used fresh strawberries, however, frozen strawberries may be substituted.

Wash a pint of fresh strawberries. Remove the stems and cut the strawberries in half. Place them in a large bowl.

☐ 2 cups FRESH STRAWBERRIES

Add the following ingredients to the bowl of strawberries.

☐ 2 cups FROZEN RHUBARB (16 oz package)

☐ 1/4 cup MINUTE TAPIOCA

☐ 1 cup SUGAR

☐ 2 tsp ORANGE RIND

Set aside for half an hour, turning once or twice. Meanwhile make a double pie crust using the recipe on page 117. Line the pie pan with the bottom crust. LATTICE the top crust (page 118).

Preheat oven to 400⁰.

Pour the fruit mixture into the unbaked bottom crust and dot with butter. ☐ 4 tsp BUTTER

Put the lattice top in place. Brush with EGG SUBSTITUTE or EVAPORATED MILK.

☐ 2 tsp EGG SUBSTITUTE (or EVAPORATED MILK))

Sprinkle the lattice crust with SUGAR.

☐ 2 tsp SUGAR

BAKING DIRECTIONS

Bake at 400⁰ for 25 minutes. Cover the pie with aluminum foil. Continue to bake for another 25 minutes, or until the crust is golden brown and the fruit bubbly.

Serve warm with VANILLA ICE CREAM.

LEMON MERINGUE PIE

You can make Lemon Meringue Pie with a lemon pudding mix, or make your own filling using the recipe on the next page.

PIE CRUST
Bake a single pie crust using the recipe on page 116.

LEMON PUDDING FILLING
Make JELLO LEMON PUDDING (not instant) according to the directions given on the package. Pour the cooked filling into the baked crust. Top with MERINGUE and bake using the directions given below.

===

MERINGUE

Have EGGS at room temperature so that they will beat to their greatest volume. Any fat will "deflate" your meringue, so start with a clean deep mixing bowl. Take a paper towel dampened with distilled white vinegar and go over the surface of the bowl and the beaters.

Beat EGG WHITES with an electric mixer. When frothy add CREAM OF TARTAR.

☐ 3 EGG WHITES   ☐ 1/2 tsp CREAM OF TARTAR

Beat on high till it forms soft peaks, then gradually add SUGAR till the meringue forms stiff peaks.

☐ 1/3 cup SUGAR

Put the meringue over the warm filling. To avoid "shrinkage," take the meringue out to the edge of the crust.

BAKING DIRECTIONS
Bake at 350° for 12-15 minutes or till meringue is golden brown. To avoid "weeping" cool to room temperature before refrigerating.

LEMON MERINGUE PIE

Anything homemade tastes best, but this Lemon Pie Filling really does taste more "lemony" and more creamy than a mix.

LEMON PIE FILING

Clean 3 to 4 lemons. Grate a tablespoon of LEMON RIND (page 211) and set aside in a small bowl.

Mix CORN STARCH INGREDIENTS in a saucepan.
CORN STARCH INGREDIENTS
- ☐ 1/4 cup WATER
- ☐ 1/3 cup CORN STARCH
- ☐ 1/2 tsp SALT

Whisk in SUGAR and WATER and cook till it comes to a boil.
- ☐ 1 cup WATER   ☐ 1 cup SUGAR

Mix EGG INGREDIENTS in a small bowl.
EGG INGREDIENTS
- ☐ 1/3 cup LEMON JUICE
- ☐ 3 EGG YOLKS

Temper the EGG INGREDIENTS by adding the hot cooked mix a tablespoon at a time into the EGG INGREDIENTS. Combine all of the ingredients in the saucepan and bring to a boil, stirring constantly. Remove from heat and stir in BUTTER and then the LEMON RIND.
- ☐ 2 TBSP BUTTER
- ☐ 1 TBSP LEMON RIND

Pour the cooked filling into a baked pie shell.
Top with MERINGUE and bake using the directions on the last page.

KEY LIME PIE

Key limes are small limes usually sold in one pound bags. They are ripe when they are yellow. Juice from a green Key Lime is bitter, no matter how much sugar is used. If the limes are green, let them ripen at room temperature until they are yellow and soft to the touch. If Key Limes are not available, substitute juice from 4 or 5 Persian Limes.

PIE CRUST
Bake a SINGLE PIE CRUST using the recipe given on page 116.

It will take the entire pound of Key Limes to squeeze a half cup of juice. To get maximum juice from this tiny fruit, place 9 in a bowl and microwave for 30 seconds. Set aside one or two limes for garnish, then microwave the rest. Strain the juice to remove pits and excess pulp.

Combine the following ingredients in a saucepan in the following order, beating with a whisk after each addition:
- [ ] 1/2 cup LIME JUICE
- [ ] 2 TBSP CORN STARCH
- [ ] 3 EGG YOLKS
- [ ] 1 can (14 oz) SWEETENED CONDENSED MILK
- [ ] 1/4 cup MILK

Cook over medium heat stirring constantly until it come to a boil. Pour the filling into the baked pie crust.

Bring to room temperature, then refrigerate several hours till set.

Make WHIPPED CREAM (page 210) with the following ingredients:
- [ ] 1/2 pint (1 cup) HEAVY WHIPPING CREAM
- [ ] 6 TBSP SUGAR

Top the pie with WHIPPED CREAM. Garnish with thin lime slices.

Custard & Cream Pies

Pumpkin Pie   134

Southern Pecan Pie   135

Coconut Custard Pie   136

Boston Cream Pie   138

Coconut Cream Pie   140

Chocolate Cream Pie   141

Banana Cream Pie   142

PUMPKIN PIE

Can't have Thanksgiving without Pumpkin Pie. This recipe is so good, you'll want to make it more than once a year.

Make an UNBAKED SINGLE PIE CRUST using the recipe on page 116. Line a 9" pie pan with the unbaked pie crust.
Brush the bottom and sides of the crust with EGG SUBSTITUTE.

- ☐ 1 TBSP EGG SUBSTITUTE

Preheat oven to 425°.
With the electric mixer on medium speed, gradually add the following ingredients in the order given.

PUMPKIN MIXTURE
- ☐ 1 3/4 cup CANNED PUMPKIN (15 oz can)
- ☐ 3/4 cup LIGHT BROWN SUGAR
- ☐ 1/2 tsp SALT
- ☐ 2/3 cup EVAPORATED MILK (5 oz can)
- ☐ 2 EGGS
- ☐ 1 tsp CINNAMON
- ☐ 1/2 tsp GINGER
- ☐ 1/4 tsp NUTMEG
- ☐ 1/8 tsp CLOVES

BAKING DIRECTIONS
Pour the PUMPKIN MIXTURE into the unbaked pie crust. Bake at 425° for 15 minutes, then cover with a silicone or metal edge protector. Reduce heat to 350°. Continue baking for 25 to 30 minute or until center is set (doesn't jiggle).
Let cool to room temperature, then refrigerate.

WHIPPED CREAM TOPPING

Serve with a spray of WHIPPED CREAM, or if you are serving a crowd, make a bowl of WHIPPED CREAM using the recipe on page 210, then each person can take as much topping as he wishes.

SOUTHERN PECAN PIE

Traditional Southern Pecan Pie is very sweet with lots of corn syrup and sugar. We reduced these ingredients for today's moderate taste. Reducing the sweetness accents the custard and pecans making this an outstanding pie. Those who crave the sugar high they remember can increase the dark corn syrup to 1 cup and the sugar to 1/2 cup.

Use the recipe on page 116 to make an UNBAKED SINGLE PIE CRUST. Line a 9" pie pan with the unbaked pie crust.
Preheat oven to 300°.

Mix PECAN HALVES with BUTTER.
- ☐ 1 cup PECAN HALVES
- ☐ 2 TBSP BUTTER (room temperature)

Arrange the BUTTERED PECANS on the bottom of the unbaked pie crust.

Break the EGGS into a bowl, then beat with a fork till blended.
- ☐ 2 EGGS

Gradually stir the following into the EGGS, in the order given.
- ☐ 2 TBSP G-F CAKE FLOUR
- ☐ 1/8 tsp SALT
- ☐ 3/4 cup DARK CORN SYRUP
- ☐ 1/3 cup SUGAR
- ☐ 1/2 tsp VANILLA

BAKING DIRECTIONS

BAKE at 300° for 50 minutes till the top is golden and the custard is set (i.e., it doesn't jiggle when moved).

You can serve the pie once it reaches room temperature, but it is best cold after several hours of refrigeration.

BOSTON CREAM PIE

Boston Cream Pie isn't really a pie. It's a layer cake, with cream filling. The story goes that the colonists baked their cakes in pie tins — sort of a one tin fits all. To give it a pie feeling, we baked the bottom layer in a cake pan and the top layer in a pie pan. Making this cake is a 4-step process:

1. Make a Vanilla Pudding Filling or a Cream Filling and put it in the refrigerator to cool.
2. While it is cooling, bake the cake.
3. Assemble the cake and then top with chocolate frosting.
4. When the chocolate is set decorate with white icing.

VANILLA PUDDING FILLING

Mix the following ingredients in a saucepan and stir over a medium heat until it comes to a boil.

- ☐ 1 package (4.6 oz) Jello Vanilla Pudding (Cook & Serve)
- ☐ 2 1/2 cups MILK (whole or 2% fat)

Refrigerate 4 or more hours until cold.

CREAM FILLING

Beat EGGS in a mixing bowl with a fork and set aside.

- ☐ 3 EGG YOLKS

Put the following ingredients in a small saucepan.

- ☐ 2/3 cup SUGAR
- ☐ 1/4 cup CORN STARCH
- ☐ 1/4 tsp SALT

Gradually add MILK and mix till blended.

- ☐ 2 cups MILK (whole or 2% fat)

Stir over low heat till it comes to a boil.

Temper the EGG YOLKS by gradually adding the cooked pudding to the beaten eggs (page 206). Once tempered, add eggs to saucepan and continue cooking and stirring until it comes to a boil. Remove from heat and stir in BUTTER and VANILLA.

- ☐ 1 TBSP BUTTER
- ☐ 1 tsp VANILLA

Refrigerate 4 or more hours until cold.

BOSTON CREAM PIE

THE CAKE

Preheat oven to 350°. Spray a 9" cake pan and a 9" pie pan.
Mix ingredients using CAKE BAKING directions on page 58.

DRY INGREDIENTS
- ☐ 1 1/2 cups G-F CAKE FLOUR
- ☐ 1 tsp XANTHAN GUM
- ☐ 2 tsp BAKING POWDER
- ☐ 1/2 tsp SALT
- ☐ 1 tsp BAKING SODA

LIQUID INGREDIENTS
- ☐ 1 cup BUTTERMILK
- ☐ 1 tsp VANILLA

SHORTENING MIX
- ☐ 1/3 cup BUTTER
- ☐ 3/4 cup SUGAR

EGGS
- ☐ 3 EGGS

BAKING DIRECTIONS

Bake at 350° for 18 to 20 minutes or till golden brown.
When the cake is at room temperature, fill with VANILLA
PUDDING FILLING or CREAM FILLING.

CHOCOLATE FROSTING

Stir ingredients in a double broiler until melted (page 204).
- ☐ 6 squares SEMI-SWEET BAKING CHOCOLATE
- ☐ 4 TBSP BUTTER ☐ 2 TBSP HEAVY CREAM

Remove from heat and stir in VANILLA.
- ☐ 1 tsp VANILLA

Frost the cake, then refrigerate for an hour to set the chocolate.

DECORATIVE ICING

Once the CHOCOLATE FROSTING is set, use the directions on
page 112 to make WHITE ICING. Make 5 circles with the icing.
Run the edge of a knife across the circles to give it a ripple
effect (see picture page 133).

COCONUT CUSTARD PIE

Creamy and crunchy all at once, this pie is a delight. It is the perfect company dessert because it is best when made the day before.

Use the recipe on page 116 to make an UNBAKED SINGLE PIE CRUST. To avoid a soggy crust, roll the pie dough an eighth of an inch thick. Use the extra dough for the outer edge of the pie crust.

Line a 9" pie pan with the unbaked pie crust.
Brush the unbaked crust with EGG SUBSTITUTE.

☐　2 tsp EGG SUBSTITUTE

Preheat oven to 425°.
Mix CUSTARD INGREDIENTS with a whisk till blended.

CUSTARD INGREDIENTS

☐　4 EGGS
☐　3/4 cup SUGAR
☐　1/2 tsp SALT
☐　1 tsp COCONUT EXTRACT

Heat milk to scalding, i.e., with small bubbles around edge.

☐　2 1/4 cups WHOLE MILK

Slowly pour the MILK over CUSTARD INGREDIENTS mixing with a spoon till blended. Pour into the unbaked pastry shell. Top with COCONUT FLAKES.

☐　2/3 cup SWEETENED COCONUT FLAKES

COCONUT CUSTARD PIE

BAKING DIRECTIONS

Bake at 425° for 10 minutes. Loosely cover the pie with aluminum foil. Reduce heat to 325° and continue to bake for 40 minutes or until center is set and doesn't jiggle when you move the pie.

Once the pie is baked, remove it from the oven and top with TOASTED COCONUT FLAKES.

TOASTED COCONUT FLAKES

Spread COCONUT FLAKES in a clean glass pie plate.

☐ 3/4 cup SWEETENED COCONUT FLAKES

Bake at 325° for 10 minutes. Once the flakes begin to turn brown, stir them with a wooden spoon. Continue baking till golden brown.

Refrigerate for several hours, or overnight, before serving.

COCONUT CREAM PIE

You can make this pie as plain for as fancy as you wish. For a plain pie, make the filling, fold in the coconut, then chill and serve. For company dessert, garnish with whipped cream and toasted coconut flakes (see picture on page 133.)

PIE CRUST

Make a BAKED SINGLE PIE CRUST using the recipe on page 116.

COCONUT CREAM FILLING

Mix CORNSTARCH and MILK in a saucepan and whisk till blended.
- ☐ 1/3 cup CORN STARCH   ☐ 1/2 cup MILK (whole or 2%)

Mix EGG YOLKS with a fork then add to saucepan.
- ☐ 3 EGG YOLKS

Gradually add rest of ingredients.
- ☐ 7 TBSP SUGAR (1/2 cup less 1 TBSP)
- ☐ 2 cups MILK (whole or 2%)   ☐ 1/2 tsp SALT

Place the saucepan over a medium heat stirring and stir till it comes to a boil. Remove from heat and stir in the following:
- ☐ 2 TBSP BUTTER   ☐ 1 tsp COCONUT EXTRACT

Once the filling is made, fold in COCONUT FLAKES
- ☐ 2/3 cup SWEETENED COCONUT FLAKES

Put filling in the baked pie crust.

GARNISH

Make WHIPPED CREAM using the recipe on page 210.
Cover the filling with the WHIPPED CREAM.

Make TOASTED COCONUT FLAKES using directions on page 139.
Sprinkle TOASTED FLAKES on top of the WHIPPED CREAM.

Favorite Desserts Made Gluten Free

CHOCOLATE CREAM PIE

Chocolate Cream Pie and the Banana Cream Pie on the next page, are pudding pies. Each can be made with a Jello Pudding mix, or with a homemade cream filling.

PIE CRUST

Make an ALMOND CRUMB CRUST using the recipe on page 120.

CHOCOLATE PUDDING FILLING

Mix the following ingredients in a saucepan.
Stir over medium heat until it comes to a boil.

- ☐ 2 packages Jello Chocolate Pudding (Cook & Serve, 3.4 oz packages)
- ☐ 2 3/4 cups MILK (whole or 2% fat)

Refrigerate till cold.

CHOCOLATE CREAM FILLING

Mix DRY INGREDIENTS in a saucepan.
DRY INGREDIENTS

- ☐ 1/3 cup CORNSTARCH
- ☐ 1/3 cup BAKING COCOA
- ☐ 1/2 tsp SALT
- ☐ 3/4 cup SUGAR

Gradually add COLD MILK and whisk till blended.

- ☐ 2 1/2 cups MILK (whole or 2% fat)

Cook over medium heat until it comes to a boil.
Remove from heat and add VANILLA ☐ 1 tsp VANILLA
Pour into baked pie crust. Refrigerate till cold.

TOPPING AND GARNISH

Make WHIPPED CREAM using the recipe on page 210.
Top the filling with WHIPPED CREAM. Garnish with SLIVERED ALMONDS. ☐ 1/4 cup SLIVERED ALMONDS

BANANA CREAM PIE

This Banana Cream Pie is like no other. It has a nutty crust and is topped with Whipped Cream and Chocolate Curls — food ecstasy for sure.

Make this recipe the order given:
CHOCOLATE CURLS
Make CHOCOLATE CURLS using the recipe on page 63.
Set aside in the refrigerator.

NUT CRUMB CRUST
Make a NUT CRUMB CRUST using the recipe on page 120.

CREAM FILLING
Make a cream filling using the recipe for VANILLA PUDDING FILLING, or CREAM FILLING (page 136). Pour cooked pudding into baked pie crust. Cool to room temperature. Cover with clear plastic and refrigerate several hours.

Before serving complete the pie with a layer of BANANAS, WHIPPED CREAM TOPPING and CHOCOLATE CURL GARNISH:
BANANA LAYER
Cut BANANAS into 1/2" circles. Mix with LEMON JUICE, then place on the VANILLA PUDDING FILLING.

☐ 2 BANANAS   ☐ 2 tsp LEMON JUICE

WHIPPED CREAM TOPPING
Make WHIPPED CREAM (page 210) with the following ingredients:

☐ 1 cup (1/2 pint) HEAVY CREAM
☐ 5 TBSP SUGAR

CHOCOLATE CURL GARNISH
Decorate with CHOCOLATE CURLS and serve.

Packaged Favorites Index

With the exception of Biscotti and "Graham" Crackers, recipes in the first part of this book are old time favorites usually baked at home. Recipes in this second part of the book are replicas of packaged treats we used to purchase at the grocery store before knowing that gluten existed.

PACKAGED COOKIES & PIES

PACKAGED CAKES

The brand names have quote marks because the given recipes are not those of the manufacturer. Though not the real thing, each Packaged Favorites recipe qualifies as a RFT (Reasonable Facsimile Thereof).

Packaged Cookies & Pies

Almond Cookie 145

Oatmeal Sandwich 146

"Oreo" 147

"Fig Newton" 148

"Moon Pie" 150

Nickel Blueberry Pie 153

Nickel Cherry Pie 153

Nickel Apple Pie 154

ALMOND COOKIE

A Chinese meal is often topped with an Almond Cookie. It is just as tasty by itself as a snack or with a glass of milk or cup of coffee.

Preheat oven to 325°. Spray two cookie sheets.
Make this cookie using the REFRIGERATOR COOKIE directions on page 25.

SHORTENING MIXTURE
- ☐ 1 EGG YOLK
- ☐ 1/3 cup BUTTER
- ☐ 1/2 cup SUGAR
- ☐ 3/4 tsp ALMOND EXTRACT

DRY INGREDIENTS
- ☐ 1 cup G-F CAKE FLOUR
- ☐ 1/4 cup ALMOND MEAL
- ☐ 1/2 tsp BAKING POWDER
- ☐ 1 tsp XANTHAN GUM
- ☐ 1/2 tsp SALT

BAKING DIRECTIONS
Cut the dough into twenty 1/4" slices.
Place 10 cookies on each cookie sheet leaving room to spread.

Beat EGG WHITE till foamy.
- ☐ 1 EGG WHITE

Brush each cookie with beaten EGG WHITE.

Press a BLANCHED ALMOND HALF in the center of each cookie.
- ☐ **20 BLANCHED ALMOND HALVES**

Bake at 325° for 25 minutes or till golden brown.
Remove from cookie sheet while warm.

OATMEAL COOKIE SANDWICH

There are gluten free rolled oats on the market at this time, but not the quick cooking oats needed for this recipe. Not a problem. Use a blender to make them quick cooking size.

Preheat oven to 350°. Liberally spray two cookie sheets.
Give the ROLLED OATS a few quick pulses in a blender.
Don't over blend. Leave some oat sized for texture.
Measure out a cup of OATS and set aside.
- ☐ 1 cup G-F ROLLED OATS (blended)

Sift and mix DRY INGREDIENTS.
DRY INGREDIENTS
- ☐ 1 cup G-F ALL PURPOSE FLOUR
- ☐ 1 tsp XANTHAN GUM
- ☐ 1/2 tsp SALT
- ☐ 1/2 tsp BAKING SODA
- ☐ 1/8 tsp NUTMEG
- ☐ 1 tsp CINNAMON
- ☐ 1/4 tsp ALLSPICE

Beat SHORTENING INGREDIENTS with an electric mixer until creamy.
SHORTENING INGREDIENTS
- ☐ 7 TBSP BUTTER (room temperature)
- ☐ 1 EGG
- ☐ 1/2 cup DARK BROWN SUGAR
- ☐ 6 TBSP SUGAR

Mix DRY INGREDIENTS into SHORTENING INGREDIENTS. Stir till blended. Add ROLLED OATS and stir till blended.

BAKING DIRECTIONS
Make 6 cookies per cookie sheet. Pat the dough into flat circles leaving room to spread. BAKE at 350° for 20 minutes or till slightly brown around the edge. Allow to cool on cookie sheet for a minute before loosening with a metal spatula.

When the cookies are room temperature, make a sandwich using the MARSHMALLOW CREAM FILLING (page 151).

THE "OREO" COOKIE

What makes a chocolate cookie an Oreo is its distinctive design. We can't replicate the design, but this cookie's naturally textured surface, rich chocolate flavor and sweet filling qualifies it as a RFT.

Follow the CUT-OUT COOKIE directions on page 50.

DRY INGREDIENTS

- ☐ 1 cup G-F ALL PURPOSE FLOUR
- ☐ 5 TBSP BAKING COCOA
- ☐ 1/2 tsp XANTHAN GUM
- ☐ 2/3 cup SUGAR
- ☐ 1/4 tsp BAKING SODA
- ☐ 1/8 tsp SALT

SHORTENING INGREDIENTS

- ☐ 3 TBSP BUTTER
- ☐ 5 TBSP MILK
- ☐ 1/2 tsp VANILLA

BAKING DIRECTIONS

Preheat the oven to 350°. Spray 2 cookie sheets.
Roll the dough thin. Use a 2" round cookie cutter or a glass rim up to 2 1/4" in diameter to make 16 cookies per cookie sheet.
Bake at 350° for 18 to 20 minutes.

"OREO" FILLING

Put EGG WHITES and WATER into a large bowl. Beat with a fork for a few minutes until the powder is absorbed.

- ☐ 1 TBSP DRIED EGG WHITES (JUST WHITES)
- ☐ 2 TBSP WARM WATER

Beat with an electric mixer till soft peaks form.
Gradually add SUGAR and VANILLA. Beat until blended.

- ☐ 2 cups SIFTED POWDERED SUGAR
- ☐ 1/4 tsp VANILLA

Place one tablespoon of filling in the middle of each cookie. Top with a cookie. Squeeze down to spread the filling to the edge.

"FIG NEWTON"

Figs are sold fresh, dried and canned. You can make a fig filling with any kind of fig. Dried figs are available year round so that was the natural choice for this recipe.

FIG FILLING

Wash 12 dried figs. Cut off and discard the small, hard, fig stems. Cover figs with water in a covered sauce pan. Simmer for 20 minutes. For a cookie with less seeds, cut the figs into quarters and then boil. Drain off water (and seeds). Pulse in blender till smooth.

Mix the FIG INGREDIENTS and set aside.

FIG INGREDIENTS

- ☐ 1 cup FIGS (cooked and blended)
- ☐ 1 tsp ORANGE RIND   ☐ 2 TBSP ORANGE JUICE
- ☐ 1/4 cup SUGAR   ☐ 2 TBSP HONEY

PASTRY DOUGH

Spray two cookie sheets. Preheat oven to 350⁰.
Sift and mix DRY INGREDIENTS.

DRY INGREDIENTS

- ☐ 1 1/2 cup G-F ALL PURPOSE FLOUR.
- ☐ 1/2 tsp BAKING POWDER
- ☐ 2 TBSP WHOLE GRAIN TEFF FLOUR
- ☐ 1 tsp XANTHAN GUM   ☐ 1/2 tsp. SALT

Mix SHORTENING INGREDIENTS till smooth.

SHORTENING INGREDIENTS

- ☐ 1/4 cup BUTTER   ☐ 1 EGG
- ☐ 1/3 cup DARK BROWN SUGAR   ☐ 1/3 cup SUGAR
- ☐ 1/2 tsp VANILLA

Add DRY INGREDIENTS to SHORTENING INGREDIENTS to form a smooth ball.

"FIG NEWTON"

ROLLING THE PASTRY DOUGH

The FIG NEWTON is essentially a filled cookie. The dough needs to be firm enough to handle. If not, refrigerate it for a half hour.

Divide the dough in half to form two balls.
— Sprinkle a silicone pie mat with RICE FLOUR.
— Put one ball of dough on the mat.
    Sprinkle the dough lightly with RICE FLOUR.
— Cover the dough with a sheet of wax paper.
— Use a rolling pin to spread the dough into a rectangle
    5" wide and 10" long.
— Use a spatula to straighten the edges.
Use the silicone mat to flip the dough onto a sprayed cookie sheet.

Repeat this procedure for the other ball of dough.

FILLING THE COOKIE

Divide the FIG FILLING in half, putting half the filling down the middle of each rectangle.
Fold the sides over the filling to form a tight seam.
Use a spatula to help turn the dough upside down on the cookie sheet, i.e., seam side down.
Pat the dough into a round, cylinder shape.
Cut the dough into 1" pieces. Do not separate till baked and cooled.

BAKING DIRECTIONS

Bake at 325° for 18 minutes. The cookie will brown slightly on the bottom, not on the top.

"MOON PIE"

I don't know where the Moon Pie got its name — maybe because it is round. It is also called a Whoopie Pie, an equally strange name. I wonder why they didn't call it a Chocolate Cookie Sandwich because that's what it is.

Preheat the oven to 350⁰. Spray 2 cookie sheets.
Sift and mix DRY INGREDIENTS.

DRY INGREDIENTS

- ☐ 1 cup G-F ALL PURPOSE FLOUR
- ☐ 1/3 cup BAKING COCOA
- ☐ 1/2 tsp BAKING SODA
- ☐ 3/4 tsp BAKING POWDER
- ☐ 1/2 tsp XANTHAN GUM
- ☐ 1/4 TSP SALT

Mix LIQUID INGREDIENTS in a bowl.

LIQUID INGREDIENTS

- ☐ 1/4 cup LIGHT OLIVE OIL   ☐ 1/2 cup MILK

EGG MIXTURE

Beat EGG with electric mixer till thick (about 5 minutes), then beat in SUGAR and VANILLA (another 5 minutes).

- ☐ 1 EGG (room temperature)
- ☐ 1/2 cup SUGAR   ☐ 1/2 tsp VANILLA

Heat **WATER** to boiling.

- ☐ 1/3 cup BOILING WATER

Add the LIQUID INGREDIENTS to the EGG MIXTURE. Fold in the DRY INGREDIENTS. Stir in the BOILING WATER till blended.

BAKING DIRECTIONS

Divide batter evenly forming 12 Moon Pies (6 per cookie sheet).
Bake at 350⁰ for 20 minutes.

Favorite Desserts Made Gluten Free

"MOON PIE"

MARSHMALLOW CREAM FILLING

Use the paddle attachment to an electric mixer to mix the following ingredients until blended.

- ☐ 2 TBSP BUTTER (room temperature)
- ☐ 2 TBSP CRISCO
- ☐ 2/3 cup MARSHMALLOW CREAM (JET-PUFFED)

Gradually add POWDERED SUGAR and VANILLA and beat till creamy.

- ☐ 1 cup POWDERED SUGAR
- ☐ 1 tsp VANILLA

ASSEMBLE THE MOON PIE

With flat top up, divide the MARSHMALLOW CREAM FILLING equally among the six pies.

Spread the filling evenly over the cookie leaving room at the edge for the filling to spread.

Place the remaining cookies on top, flat side covering the filling.

THE NICKEL PIE

They were called Nickel Pies, cause that's what they cost. I remember apple, blueberry, cherry and peach. Fruit pies are available today — though they cost more than a nickel and come in a rectangular shape. To make this old time favorite, you need 6" pie pans. Six inch ceramic pie pans are available in baking supply stores, but the better choice is a 6" aluminum foil pie pans sold at some supermarkets.

You might think baking a Nickel Pie is the same as baking a regular pie, only on a smaller scale. Not so. Regular fruit pies are stuffed with as much fruit as the pastry shell will hold. The Nickel Pie is flat on top with lots of sweet filling. A solution would be to use canned pie filling, if only they didn't contain modified food starch (another name for gluten). There are canned fruits on the market that contain fruit packed in water or light syrup and that is what we used to make these Nickel Pies.

THE NICKEL PIE CRUST

Follow the PIE CRUST directions (page 114).

SHORTENING ☐ 6 TBSP CRISCO

LIQUID INGREDIENTS
☐ 1 1/4 tsp WHITE VINEGAR ☐ 1 1/4 tsp EGG SUBSTITUTE
☐ 2 TBSP ICE WATER

DRY INGREDIENTS
☐ 1 1/3 cups G-F ALL PURPOSE FLOUR ☐ 1/2 tsp SALT
☐ 1 tsp XANTHAN GUM

ADDITIONAL WATER ☐ Up to 3 TBSP COLD WATER

Divide dough into 4 equal parts. Roll out 2 bottom crusts. Place a crust in each pie pan. Roll out 2 top crusts and set each aside. Complete the pie using one of the fruit recipes on the next two pages.

NICKEL PIE FILLING DIRECTIONS

Strain the liquid of a can of FRUIT into a small saucepan. Set the fruit aside in a bowl. Add the FILLING INGREDIENTS to the liquid in the saucepan. Cook over a medium heat stirring constantly with a whisk. Once the filling comes to a boil, remove from heat and pour over the fruit. Divide the fruit and filling equally between the two unbaked pie shells.

Place the top crust over the filling. Use a fork to make an initial in the crust, e.g. "B" for blueberry, "C" for cherry.

Brush the top crust with EGG SUBSTITUTE.

☐ 2 tsp EGG SUBSTITUTE

BAKING DIRECTIONS

Bake the pie at 375° for 35 minutes or till crust is golden brown and the filling bubbly.

NICKEL BLUEBERRY PIE

Follow the NICKEL PIE CRUST and NICKEL PIE FILLING directions with the following ingredients:

FRUIT ☐ 1 can (15 oz) BLUEBERRIES packed in light syrup

FILLING INGREDIENTS

☐ 1 1/2 TBSP CORN STARCH   ☐ 5 TBSP SUGAR
☐ 1 TBSP LEMON JUICE   ☐ 1/8 tsp SALT

NICKEL CHERRY PIE

Follow the NICKEL PIE CRUST and NICKEL PIE FILLING directions with the following ingredients:

FRUIT ☐ 1 can (15 oz) RED TART CHERRIES packed in water

FILLING INGREDIENTS

☐ 1 1/2 TBSP CORN STARCH   ☐ 6 TBSP SUGAR
☐ 1 TBSP ORANGE JUICE   ☐ 1/8 tsp SALT

THE NICKEL APPLE PIE

Canned apples come in 20 oz cans. That's enough for three Nickel Pies. You can make two pies, however they will have full rounded crusts making them mini apple pies. We adjusted the ingredients for the pie crust to make 3 Nickel Pies, so you have your choice of making three Nickel Apple Pies or two Mini Apple Pies.

CRUST FOR 2 NICKEL APPLE PIES

Make two double pie crusts using the recipe on page 152.

CRUST FOR 3 NICKEL APPLE PIES

Make three double pie crusts using the recipe for a SINGLE PIE CRUST on page 116.

FILLING DIRECTIONS FOR 2 OR 3 APPLE PIES

Drain the liquid from a can of APPLES into a saucepan.
☐ 1 can (20 oz) APPLES (packed in water)
Put the apples aside in a bowl.

Add the FILLING INGREDIENTS to the canned liquid.
Stir over medium heat till it comes to a boil.

FILLING INGREDIENTS

☐ 2 1/2 TBSP CORN STARCH   ☐ 3 TBSP ORANGE JUICE
☐ 1/4 cup BROWN SUGAR   ☐ 3 TBSP SUGAR
☐ 1 tsp CINNAMON   ☐ 1/8 tsp SALT

Add the cooked filling to the apples. Divide the apples and apple filling into the unbaked pie shells (2 pie shells for the mini apple pie, 3 for the Nickel Apple Pie). Cover the fruit with the top crust. Brush top crusts with EGG SUBSTITUTE.
☐ 1 TBSP EGG SUBSTITUTE

BAKING DIRECTIONS

Bake the pie at 375° for 40 minutes or till crust is golden brown and the filling is bubbly.

Packaged Cakes

"Hostess Cup Cake" 157

"Twinkie" 158

"Sno Ball" 160

Jelly Roll 162

Crumb Cake 164

"Tastykake" 166

VANILLA FILLING

We start this section with Vanilla Filling because the first three recipes in this section "Hostess Cupcake", "Twinkie" and "Sno Ball" use this filling.

VANILLA FILLING

Beat the SHORTENING INGREDIENTS with the whisk attachment to an electric mixer till blended.

SHORTENING INGREDIENTS

☐ 1 TBSP CRISCO
☐ 2 TBSP BUTTER (room temperature)
☐ 1 1/3 cup POWDERED SUGAR
☐ 1/2 tsp VANILLA

With mixer on high, drizzle SYRUP into SHORTENING and beat for 5 minutes.

SYRUP

☐ 3 TBSP LIGHT CORN SYRUP

FILLING THE CUPCAKE

Put the VANILLA FILLING in a pastry bag with a thin nozzle. Squeeze a teaspoon of filling in each cupcake. Practice squeezing the bag to get the feel of a teaspoon of filling.

THE EASY WAY

I must admit, I never quite got the hang of a pastry bag. I usually end up with more filling on me than in the cupcake. So I do it the easy way. I cut the cupcake in half horizontally, scoop out a teaspoon of cake. Replace the missing cake with filling. Replace the top (and no one the wiser).

"HOSTESS CUPCAKE"

This popular cupcake is instantly recognizable with its shiny chocolate frosting and ringlet icing.

CHOCOLATE CUPCAKES

Preheat oven to 350°. Spray a 12 cup cupcake pan.

Use the whisk attachment to an electric mixer to beat EGGS for 10 minutes. Add SUGAR and beat another 5 minutes.

- ☐ 1 EGG + 1 EGG WHITE
- ☐ 2/3 cup SUGAR

Meanwhile, sift and mix DRY INGREDIENTS.

DRY INGREDIENTS

- ☐ 1 cup G-F CAKE FLOUR
- ☐ 1 tsp BAKING POWDER
- ☐ 1/2 tsp XANTHAN GUM
- ☐ 1/3 cup BAKING COCOA
- ☐ 1/2 tsp BAKING SODA
- ☐ 1/4 tsp SALT

Mix LIQUID INGREDIENTS in a bowl.

LIQUID INGREDIENTS

- ☐ 1/4 cup LIGHT OLIVE OIL
- ☐ 1/2 tsp VANILLA
- ☐ 9 TBSP (1/2 cup + 1 TBSP) MILK (whole or 2% fat)

Alternate DRY and LIQUID INGREDIENTS into EGG MIXTURE (page 57).

BAKING DIRECTIONS

Bake at 350° for 25 minutes. Let the cupcakes reach room temperature in the pan. While in the pan, cut off the rounded cap so the cupcake will sit flat when turned upside-down. Set the caps aside. Make the VANILLA FILLING recipe on the last page. Use it to fill the cupcakes. Use the leftover FILLING to make 6 cupcake cap "sandwiches."

Turn the cupcakes upside-down. Use the GLOSSY CHOCOLATE FROSTING recipe on page 39 to frost the cupcake. Let the frosting set for an hour. Use WHITE ICING (page 112) to make the signature Hostess ringlet design on top of the cupcake.

"TWINKIE"

SPECIAL EQUIPMENT

The thing that identifies a Twinkie, is its oblong shape. We baked this treat using a special oblong shaped muffin pan. It came as part of a Twinkie Bake Set that I purchased some time ago. It was one of my better purchases. The set contained a baking pan with an 8 cup Twinkie shaped muffin pan, a pastry bag with long nozzle and a recipe book. I use the baking pan to make frankfurter rolls, as well as Twinkies and other desserts. The plastic pastry bag is great for decorating cakes. I used the recipe book as the starting point for creating gluten free Twinkies.

I don't know if the company still markets the Twinkie Bake Set. You can check their web site to see if it is available. If you do not have a oblong muffin pan, use a square pan (8" X 8" X 2") and cut the cake into 8 rectangular cakes.

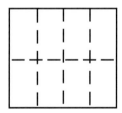

"TWINKIE"

MIXING THE TWINKIE BATTER

The Twinkie batter is made the same as a cake batter.
See page 58 for detailed cake baking directions.

Preheat the oven and spray the baking pan.
Sift and mix the DRY INGREDIENTS.

DRY INGREDIENTS

- ☐ 1 cup G-F CAKE FLOUR
- ☐ 1/2 tsp BAKING SODA
- ☐ 1/4 tsp SALT
- ☐ 1/2 tsp XANTHAN GUM
- ☐ 1/2 tsp BAKING POWDER

Combine LIQUID INGREDIENTS in another bowl.

LIQUID INGREDIENTS

- ☐ 2/3 cup MILK
- ☐ 3/4 tsp VANILLA

Beat the BUTTER and SUGAR till creamy. Gradually beat in EGGS.

SHORTENING INGREDIENTS

- ☐ 1/4 cup BUTTER
- ☐ 2 EGGS + 1 EGG WHITE
- ☐ 2/3 cup SUGAR

Alternate DRY and LIQUID INGREDIENTS into the SHORTENING INGREDIENTS (page 57).

BAKING DIRECTIONS

Bake in a slow oven 325⁰ for 12 to 15 minutes or till light brown.
Let the cakes come to room temperature in the pan.

FILLING THE TWINKIE

Make the VANILLA FILLING recipe on 156.
While the cakes are in the pan, fill 3 holes in the top.
Once filled, remove them from the pan and turn the TWINKIES upside-down to serve. See the pictures on page 155 for top and bottom view of the TWINKIE.

"SNO BALL"

The Hostess Sno Ball is a chocolate cupcake, with vanilla filling, covered with a marshmallow-coconut frosting. Sno Balls can be white, or pink, or any color you wish. To color the coconut flakes, put a few drops of food coloring into the blender as you shred the coconut.

Preheat oven to 350°. Spray a 12 cup muffin pan.

EGG INGREDIENTS

☐ 2 EGGS   ☐ 3/4 cup SUGAR

Beat EGGS for 10 minutes with the whisk attachment of an electric mixer. Gradually beat in SUGAR and beat on high for another 5 minutes.

Meanwhile, sift and mix DRY INGREDIENTS.

DRY INGREDIENTS

☐ 1 1/4 cups G-F CAKE FLOUR
☐ 6 TBSP BAKING COCOA   ☐ 1/4 tsp SALT
☐ 1 tsp XANTHAN GUM   ☐ 1/2 tsp BAKING SODA
☐ 1 1/4 tsp BAKING POWDER

Combine LIQUID INGREDIENTS in a bowl and set aside.

LIQUID INGREDIENTS

☐ 2/3 cup MILK   ☐ 3/4 tsp VANILLA
☐ 1/3 cup LIGHT OLIVE OIL

Alternate DRY INGREDIENTS and LIQUID INGREDIENTS into EGG INGREDIENTS (page 57).

BAKING DIRECTIONS

Divide batter evenly into the muffin pan. Each cup will fill almost to the top to give the cupcake maximum ball effect as it bakes.

Bake at 350° for 25 to 30 minutes.

"SNO BALL"

VANILLA FILLING

The MARSHMALLOW TOPPING is so rich and delicious, that the VANILLA FILLING is optional. Still, if you wish to be faithful to the packaged Sno Ball make he VANILLA FILLING recipe on page 156. You can fill the cupcake from the bottom or the top — or the easy way.

COCONUT FLAKES

Put **COCONUT FLAKES** in a blender and shred into small flakes.

☐ **2 cups SWEETENED COCONUT FLAKES**

To color the COCONUT put 2 to 3 drops of food coloring into the Coconut as it is being shredded. Set aside.

MARSHMALLOW TOPPING

Make the topping with the MARSHMALLOW recipe on page 40. As soon as the topping is finished beating, use a spatula to frost the sides and rounded top of the cupcake. Use all of the Marshmallow recipe piling it high on the cupcake.

The Marshmallow Topping will begin to set in a few minutes, so press the shredded COCONUT FLAKES into the topping as you frost each cupcake.

JELLY ROLL

This dessert looks harder to make than it is. The trick is to follow the ROLLING DIRECTIONS given on the next page. You'll be surprised how professional the finished Jelly Roll looks.

Use the whisk attachment of an electric mixer to beat the EGG INGREDIENTS for 15 minutes.

EGG INGREDIENTS
- ☐ 3 EGGS (room temperature)
- ☐ 1/2 tsp CREAM OF TARTAR

Gradually add SUGAR and VANILLA and continue beating for another 5 minutes.

- ☐ 2/3 cup SUGAR
- ☐ 1 tsp VANILLA

Meanwhile line an insulated cookie sheet (15"" x 10 x 1 3/8") with parchment paper (page 206).
Preheat oven to 350°.

Sift and mix DRY INGREDIENTS.

DRY INGREDIENTS
- ☐ 1 1/4 cup G-F CAKE FLOUR
- ☐ 1/4 tsp SALT
- ☐ 1 tsp BAKING POWDER
- ☐ 1 tsp XANTHAN GUM

Heat MILK to a simmer.

- ☐ 1/2 cup MILK (whole milk or 2% fat)

Fold DRY INGREDIENTS into EGG MIXTURE, then fold in hot MILK.

BAKING DIRECTIONS
Pour onto the lined cookie sheet.
Bake at 350° for 15 minutes or till light brown.

JELLY ROLL

ROLLING DIRECTIONS

Liberally dust a clean dish towel (15' X 10") with POWDERED SUGAR.

☐   **1/2 cup POWDERED SUGAR**

While hot from the oven, turn the cake onto the powdered towel.
Peel off the parchment paper.
Roll cake lengthwise (i.e. 15" side) using towel as a guide.

Wrap towel around roll to help keep its shape as it cools.
Let cool for 10 minutes on a wire rack.

Empty the preserves into a small bowl.

☐   **1 cup RASPBERRY PRESERVES**
       (with or without seeds)

Mash with a fork to make the preserves smooth and easy to spread.

Gently unwind the jelly roll and spread with a thin layer of preserves (about half a cup).
Spread the preserves out to within a half inch of the edge.
Rewind the jelly roll.
Spread the remaining preserves over the outside of the jelly roll.

Sprinkle the preserves with COCONUT FLAKES.

☐   **2/3 cup of SWEETENED COCONUT FLAKES**

CRUMB CAKE

Who can resist a packaged Crumb Cake? Some are sold as rectangular cakes — others as Crumb Cake "pies". We used two muffin cap pans to bake "pies."

If you do not have muffin cap pans, bake in a rectangular pan (9" x 12"). When room temperature cut into 12 squares (each 3" X 3") by dividing the 9" side into thirds and the 12" side into quarters.

Start the recipe by making the CRUMB TOPPING.

CRUMB TOPPING

Sift and mix the DRY INGREDIENTS.
DRY INGREDIENTS
- [ ] 1/4 cup SUGAR
- [ ] 1/4 cup DARK BROWN SUGAR
- [ ] 1 cup G-F ALL PURPOSE FLOUR
- [ ] 1/4 tsp SALT
- [ ] 1/4 tsp NUTMEG
- [ ] 1/2 tsp CINNAMON

Cut the BUTTER into the DRY INGREDIENTS (page 208).
- [ ] 5 TBSP BUTTER (cold from the refrigerator)

Work the dough with your fingers until it forms a ball. Crumble the ball into 1/2" crumbs and set aside.

CRUMB CAKE

The Crumb Cake is mixed the same as a cake. See page 58 for detailed cake baking directions.

Preheat the oven to 350°. Spray the baking pan(s).

Sift and mix the DRY INGREDIENTS.

DRY INGREDIENTS

- ☐ 1 cup G-F CAKE FLOUR
- ☐ 3/4 tsp XANTHAN GUM
- ☐ 1/2 tsp BAKING SODA
- ☐ 1/2 tsp BAKING POWDER
- ☐ 1/2 tsp EGG REPLACER
- ☐ 1/4 tsp SALT

Combine the LIQUID INGREDIENTS in another bowl.

LIQUID INGREDIENTS

- ☐ 1/2 cup MILK (whole or 2% Fat)
- ☐ 1/2 tsp VANILLA

Beat the BUTTER and SUGAR till creamy.

SHORTENING INGREDIENTS

- ☐ 1/4 cup BUTTER   ☐ 1/2 cup SUGAR

Gradually beat in EGGS.

EGGS   ☐ 2 EGGS

Alternate DRY and LIQUID INGREDIENTS into SHORTENING INGREDIENTS (page 57).

Divide cake batter equally into the two muffin cap pans.

Spread the CRUMB TOPPING evenly over the cake batter.

BAKING DIRECTIONS

Bake at 350° for 20 minutes or till sides are golden brown.

Once the CRUMB CAKES are room temperature, dust with POWDERED SUGAR and serve.

- ☐ 1/4 cup POWDERED SUGAR

"TASTYKAKE "

Tastykakes were my favorite childhood treat. They came three to a package. Normally, a generous child — not with these chocolate delights. I would down all of them. No thought of sharing.

Make 12 cupcakes using the CHOCOLATE CUPCAKE recipe on page 157.

Let the cupcake cool to room temperature in the pan. The cupcake is frosted on the bottom to get that flat Tastykake look. To make the cupcake sit flat when turned upside-down cut off the rounded cupcake cap with a thin sharp, knife.

CHOCOLATE FROSTING

Mix the SUGAR INGREDIENTS together with spoon till blended.
SUGAR INGREDIENTS
- ☐ 4 1/2 TBSP MILK
- ☐ 1 1/2 TBSP LIGHT CORN SYRUP
- ☐ 3 TBSP BAKING COCOA
- ☐ 2 1/4 cups POWDERED SUGAR
- ☐ 3/4 tsp VANILLA

Melt the BAKING CHOCOLATE in a micro oven (page 209).
- ☐ 1 1/2 squares SEMI-SWEET BAKING CHOCOLATE

Beat the melted chocolate into the SUGAR INGREDIENTS with a hand held mixer.

Frost the cupcakes, then place them on a wire rack for an hour to set.

Of course, there's no harm in eating the cupcake while the frosting is still soft.

Bakery Favorites Index

This final section of the book contains recipes for bakery treats — desserts not usually baked at home. This last section is challenging because it builds on the skills developed earlier (i.e., making cookies, pies and cakes). If you are new to baking, you may want to make a recipe from the first part of this book before trying one of these Bakery Favorites.

PASTRIES

These pastries are sold at fine bakeries, or served at upscale restaurants.

DELI FAVORITES

Deli Favorites are cookies and pastries sold in the bakery section of a delicatessen.

Pastries

Charlotte Russe   169

Lady Fingers   170

Tiramisu   172

Petit Four   174

Cream Puffs   176

Eclair   178

Empanadas   179

Napoleon   180

CHARLOTTE RUSSE

Charlotte Russe was sold in New York in the mid 1900's. It came in a cardboard cupcake container with a moveable bottom so that the sponge cake could be pushed up as the top mound of whipped cream was eaten. I could not find push up containers, but a cupcake liner works as well. The whipped cream can be eaten down, and the liner peeled away to reach the cake. This recipe makes 24 cupcakes. It is a great company dessert. Elegant, yet easy to make.

Bring EGGS to room temperature. Beat EGG MIXTURE for 15 minutes using the whisk attachment to an electric mixer.
EGG MIXTURE ☐ 2 EGGS ☐ 1/4 tsp CREAM OF TARTAR
Gradually add SUGAR MIXTURE and beat another 5 minutes.
SUGAR MIXTURE ☐ 5 TBSP SUGAR ☐ 1/2 tsp VANILLA

Meanwhile, preheat oven to 375°.
Put cupcake liners into two 12 cup muffin pans.
DRY INGREDIENTS
☐ 6 TBSP G-F CAKE FLOUR ☐ 1/8 tsp SALT
Mix DRY INGREDIENTS, then fold into beaten EGGS.
Heat MILK in micro for 20 seconds, then blend into batter.
☐ 2 TBSP MILK (whole or 2% fat)
BAKING DIRECTIONS
Divide batter evenly into the 24 cups (one tablespoon per cup).
Bake at 375° for 10 minutes.

CREAM AND CHERRY TOPPING
Make WHIPPED CREAM with the following ingredients (page 210).
☐ 2 pints (4 cups) HEAVY CREAM
☐ 1 1/2 cup SUGAR ☐ 2 tsp VANILLA
Drain CHERRIES on a paper towel.
☐ 24 MARASCHINO CHERRIES (with stems)
Use a pastry bag to top the sponge cake high with WHIPPED CREAM. Place a CHERRY on top of each cupcake.

LADY FINGERS

A Trifle is a layered dessert served in a large glass bowl so that all of the layers of cake, cream filling, and fruit, can be seen. The cake is one that readily absorbs fruit juices such as a sponge cake or a pound cake. Lady Fingers are a favorite choice because they can be purchased at the supermarket. Then all the cook needs to do is layer them with filling and fresh fruit. We don't have the luxury of buying a package of Lady Fingers, so we start with that recipe.

Line 2 large cookie sheets with parchment paper (page 206).

Beat the EGG YOLK INGREDIENTS for 15 minutes using the whisk attachment of an electric mixer. If you don't have a counter top electric mixer, use a hand held mixer and wash the beaters before beating the EGG WHITE INGREDIENTS.

EGG YOLK INGREDIENTS
- ☐ 3 EGG YOLKS
- ☐ 1/2 tsp VANILLA
- ☐ 1/4 cup SUGAR

Meanwhile, sift and mix DRY INGREDIENTS and set aside in a small bowl.

DRY INGREDIENTS
- ☐ 1/4 cup RICE FLOUR
- ☐ 2 TBSP POTATO STARCH
- ☐ 1/4 tsp XANTHAN GUM
- ☐ 1 TBSP TAPIOCA STARCH
- ☐ 1/8 tsp SALT

EGG WHITE INGREDIENTS
- ☐ 3 EGG WHITES
- ☐ 1/2 tsp CREAM OF TARTAR

Beat EGG WHITES till foamy, then add the CREAM OF TARTAR. Continue to beat on high speed, until it forms firm peaks.

Fold the DRY INGREDIENTS into the beaten EGG YOLKS, then fold in the beaten EGG WHITES.

LADY FINGERS

Form 4" X 1" strips by dropping the batter onto the parchment with a large serving size spoon. Make each strip 1" high. Add a second layer of batter if necessary. Use a butter knife or spatula to help shape the Lady Fingers. Make 8 Lady Fingers per cookie sheet. Leave room for spreading.

Sift and mix SUGARS.

SUGARS
- ☐ 3 TBSP POWDERED SUGAR
- ☐ 2 tsp SUGAR

Sift half of the SUGARS over the Lady Fingers.
Let stand 10 minutes.

Preheat the oven to 350°.
Sprinkle the remaining SUGARS over the Lady Fingers and let stand another 5 minutes.

BAKING DIRECTIONS

Bake for 10 minutes at 350°, then rotate the cookie sheets (bottom to top rack and top to bottom rack) to allow the Lady Fingers to brown evenly.
Bake another 5 to 8 minutes till slightly brown. Don't overbake.

Let the Lady Fingers cool on the parchment paper, then peel from the paper.

SERVING THE LADY FINGERS

Lady Fingers are delicious all by themselves, or you can make pastry sandwiches by putting orange marmalade, or apricot preserves on the flat side of the cookie and topping it with the flat side of another Lady Finger. Better yet, use the recipe on the next page to make TIRAMISU.

TIRAMISU

Tiramisu is an Italian Trifle. It is made with Mascarpone (an Italian cream cheese) mixed with beaten eggs. Problem is, the food police in my neighborhood have long since banned the eating of raw eggs. In addition, Mascarpone is expensive and not available in all parts of the country. We substituted cream cheese, ricotta cheese and a bit of sour cream. This recipe may not be authentic Tiramisu, but it looks the same and tastes great.

Bring cheeses to room temperature.
Make LADY FINGERS using the recipe on page 170.
- ☐ 16 LADY FINGERS

Beat the CHEESE INGREDIENTS till smooth.
CHEESE INGREDIENTS
- ☐ 2/3 cup SUGAR
- ☐ 8 oz package CREAM CHEESE**
- ☐ 3 TBSP RICOTTA CHEESE**
- ☐ 1 TBSP SOUR CREAM **

**For an authentic tasting Tiramisu, use original formula CREAM CHEESE, RICOTTA CHEESE and SOUR CREAM. Not low fat.

Stir COFFEE INGREDIENTS till blended.
COFFEE INGREDIENTS
- ☐ 1/4 cup BOILING WATER
- ☐ 1 TBSP SUGAR
- ☐ 1 TBSP COFFEE GRANULES
- ☐ 1 TBSP BAKING COCOA

Place the LADY FINGERS on a cookie sheet flat side up.
Brush the flat side with the COFFEE mixture.

TIRAMISU

FORMING THE CAKE

Line a loaf pan 5 X 9" X 3" with plastic wrap. Arrange the Lady Fingers on the bottom of the loaf pan with flat (coffee) side facing up. You may need to cut a few Lady Fingers in half to make them fit across the bottom.

Line the sides with the Lady Fingers flat side facing inward.

Top the bottom layer with half of the CHEESE INGREDIENTS. Put a layer of Lady Fingers on top of the Cheese layer, flat side facing upward. Top with the other half of the CHEESE INGREDIENTS. Top with another layer of Lady Fingers flat side facing downward.

Once the TIRAMISU is set, it will be turned upside-down on a plate. The last layer of LADY FINGERS will become the bottom of the cake so it is important that the last layer is even with the top of sides. If the sides are too long, cut the Lady Fingers to fit.

Cover with plastic wrap and refrigerate overnight.

Make WHIPPED CREAM using the recipe on page 210.

Turn the cake upside-down onto a plate.
Remove the plastic wrap.
Cover the top and sides with WHIPPED CREAM.

CHOCOLATE SHAVINGS

Run a potato peeler along the side of a bar of SEMI-SWEET BAKING CHOCOLATE to make CHOCOLATE SHAVINGS.

Sprinkle the top of the cake with the shavings and serve.

PETIT FOUR

A Petit Four is a small, frosted and decorated, cake. Most people think that only a skilled French pastry chef can create this delicate pastry. But it is not as hard as it looks. Bake a thin sheet cake, cut it into shapes, then use your imagination to decorate. Frosting the Petit Fours takes time so make them the day before serving to company.

LEMON SHEET CAKE

Bring EGGS and BUTTER to room temperature.
Line a cookie sheet (10" X 15" X 1 3/8") with parchment (page 206).
Preheat over to 350°. Use the whisk attachment to an electric mixer to beat EGG MIXTURE INGREDIENTS for 20 minutes.

EGG INGREDIENTS
- ☐ 2 EGGS + 1 EGG WHITE
- ☐ 1/2 tsp CREAM OF TARTAR

Meanwhile, sift and mix DRY INGREDIENTS.

DRY INGREDIENTS
- ☐ 1 1/4 cup G-F CAKE FLOUR
- ☐ 1 tsp BAKING POWDER
- ☐ 1/2 tsp BAKING SODA
- ☐ 1/2 tsp SALT
- ☐ 1 tsp XANTHAN GUM
- ☐ 1 tsp GELATIN

Beat SHORTENING INGREDIENTS till creamy.

SHORTENING INGREDIENTS
- ☐ 1/2 cup SUGAR
- ☐ 1 tsp LEMON RIND
- ☐ 1/3 cup BUTTER
- ☐ 1 TBSP LEMON JUICE

Add beaten EGGS to SHORTENING. Stir till blended.
Fold in DRY INGREDIENTS till blended. Heat MILK till simmering.
- ☐ 1/2 cup MILK (whole or 2% fat)

Add the HOT MILK to the batter. Stir till well blended.

BAKING DIRECTIONS

Pour the batter onto the parchment. Use a spatula to level and smooth the top of the batter. Bake at 350° for 15 minutes or until golden brown and the cake pulls away from the sides.

PETIT FOUR

FORMING THE PETIT FOUR

Once the cake is room temperature, remove the parchment paper. Cut the cake into circles, hearts — any shape your cutters and imagination allow. The cake makes 15 two layer Petit Fours with scraps left over. For an easy and economical way, cut the cake into 5 equal parts horizontally and 8 parts vertically making 20 two layers Petit Fours each 2" X 1.9".

FILLING THE PETIT FOUR

Layer the cakes by placing a teaspoon of preserves as a filling. Orange Marmalade, Fruit Preserves, Mint Jelly, all work well. Once the cake is filled, cover it with a THIN GLAZE to set the shape and keep crumbs out of the frosting.

THIN GLAZE

☐ 2 cups POWDERED SUGAR   ☐ 3 TBSP WATER

Beat the POWDERED SUGAR and WATER together till smooth. Cover cake with the glaze. Let glaze set for an hour.

PETIT FOUR FROSTING

CHEFMASTER is a meringue powder sold by KING ARTHUR FLOUR The ROYAL ICING recipe on the label is easy to make and works well as a Petit Four frosting. If you don't have CHEFMASTER, make the FLUFFY WHITE FROSTING on page 61, only increase the POWDERED SUGAR to 4 cups for a firmer consistency. Eliminate the VANILLA EXTRACT — unless you want vanilla flavoring for all of the Petit Fours.

COLORING THE FROSTING

Work with one cup of frosting at a time. Add a few drops of coloring and 1/4 tsp of flavoring. For example, to make lemon Petit Fours, add a few drops of yellow and 1/4 tsp LEMON EXTRACT.

THE GARNISH

Before the frosting hardens, garnish the cake. Coconut flakes, cherries, nuts, decorative sugar, orange zest all work well.

CREAM PUFFS

The Cream Puff is an airy, cream-filled pastry. The filling can be a Vanilla Pudding Filling (page 138) or a Chocolate Pudding Filling (page 141) or a Whipped Cream Filling (page 210) or the following Cream Puff Filling.

CREAM PUFF FILLING

Put the following ingredients in a saucepan.

- [ ] 1/2 cup SUGAR
- [ ] 3 TBSP CORN STARCH
- [ ] 1/2 tsp SALT

Gradually add MILK. Stir till blended.

- [ ] 2 cups MILK (whole or 2% fat)

Beat EGGS YOLKS till blended, then use a whisk to mix them into the saucepan. Stir till the YOLKS are no longer visible.

- [ ] 2 EGG YOLKS

Stir over medium heat until it comes to a boil.

Remove from heat and mix BUTTER and VANILLA.

- [ ] 1 1/2 TBSP BUTTER
- [ ] 1 tsp VANILLA.

Pour into a bowl, cool to room temperature, cover with plastic wrap and refrigerate for 4 or more hours.

CREAM PUFFS

CREAM PUFF PASTRY

Spray 2 cookie sheets. Preheat oven to 450°.
Sift and mix DRY INGREDIENTS.

DRY INGREDIENTS

- ☐ 1/3 cup POTATO STARCH
- ☐ 1/2 TSP XANTHAN GUM
- ☐ 1 TBSP SUGAR
- ☐ 2/3 cup RICE FLOUR
- ☐ 1/2 tsp SALT

Put SHORTENING INGREDIENTS in a saucepan. Cook till it comes to a boil and the shortening is melted.

SHORTENING INGREDIENTS

- ☐ 1/2 cup CRISCO
- ☐ 1 cup WATER

Add DRY INGREDIENTS to SHORTENING INGREDIENTS all at once. Stir with wooden spoon till blended. Transfer dough to an electric mixer with paddle attachment.
Beat in EGGS one at a time.

EGGS

- ☐ 3 EGGS + 1 EGG WHITE

Drop dough by rounded tablespoon onto the cookie sheets making 6 cream puffs per sheet each 2" round and 2" high.

BAKING DIRECTIONS

Bake at 450° for 15 minutes.
Reduce heat to 325° and bake for 10 minutes till golden brown. Turn off the oven and let them remain in the oven for another 10 minutes.

Place Cream Puffs on a wire rack to cool. Make a small slit in one of the creases of the cream puff to allow the steam to escape. When room temperature, cut the cream puff along one of the baking creases. Remove any "gummy" dough.
Fill with a cream or pudding filling, then replace the "cap."
Dust with POWDERED SUGAR and serve.

ECLAIR

The Eclair is the companion dessert to the Cream Puff. They are both made from the same pastry dough. You can use one cookie sheet to make 6 Cream Puffs and the other to make 5 Eclairs or use this recipe to make 10 Eclairs.

ECLAIR FILLING

Make the CREAM PUFF FILLING using the recipe on page 176.

ECLAIR PASTRY

Make the dough using the recipe on page 177. Use a pastry bag with just the nozzle and no attachment. Squeeze out a strip of dough 6" long and 1 " wide. Squeeze out another strip on top of the first strip, making a strip 6" long and 2" high.
Make 5 Eclairs per cookie sheet. Leave room to spread.

Bake and cool the Eclair as directed on the last page. Cut the Eclair in half along the horizontal crease. Scoop out any "gummy" dough. Cover the top half with CHOCOLATE GLAZE.

CHOCOLATE GLAZE

Heat HEAVY CREAM in a bowl in the micro for 30 seconds.
☐ 1/3 cup HEAVY CREAM
Stir in SUGAR and VANILLA.
☐ 1/2 cup POWDERED SUGAR   ☐ 1 tsp VANILLA

Heat CHOCOLATE in micro till melted (page 209).
☐ 3 squares SEMI-SWEET BAKING CHOCOLATE
Beat melted CHOCOLATE into HEAVY CREAM mixture.
Spread the GLAZE on top of the Eclair with a butter knife.

Fill the bottom half of the Eclair with the CREAM PUFF FILLING, then cover with the glazed top half.
Refrigerate for an hour to set the CHOCOLATE GLAZE.

EMPANADAS

Empanadas are Mexican turnovers. They are made with pie crust dough, rolled thin. They can be fried or baked. They can be made with a savory or sweet filling. Many other countries have a sweet turnover as a traditional dessert, so we included this recipe in the Pastry section. We used Cherry Preserves, but Empanadas can be filled with any of the following:

- ☐ crushed pineapple mixed with coconut flakes
- ☐ chunky apple sauce mixed with chopped nuts
- ☐ raisins and nuts mixed with jelly
- ☐ mincemeat
- ☐ fruit preserves

Preheat the oven to 350°. Spray two cookie sheets.
Make the recipe for a SINGLE PIE CRUST on page 116.
Divide the dough into two halves.
Roll out one of the halves. Use a 3" biscuit cutter, or the 3" rim of a glass to cut the dough into 10 circles.
Place the circles onto a sprayed cookie sheet.
Repeat with the remaining dough, making a total of 20 pastries.

Put 1 level teaspoonful of filling in the middle of each pastry.
FILLING   ☐ 1/2 cup CHERRY PRESERVES
Moisten the edges with water. Fold the pastry in half into a turnover shape. Use a fork to seal the edges.

Brush each pastry with EGG SUBSTITUTE.
              ☐   2 TBSP EGG SUBSTITUTE

BAKING DIRECTIONS
Bake at 350° for 20 minutes, till filling is bubbly and crust golden brown.
Sprinkle liberally with POWDERED SUGAR and serve.

NAPOLEON

The Napoleon is a French Pastry with layers of puff pastry and cream filling. Gluten free puff pastry is not currently on the market. We used a dough similar to Cream Puff dough for a RFT. This is one of those challenging recipes we spoke of in the Introduction to this book. It has multi-steps and dough that is not easy to handle. Still, if you yearn for a Napoleon, this will more than satisfy.

Make a double recipe of the CREAM PUFF FILLING on page 176 or for special treat make a single CREAM PUFF FILLING recipe for one layer and CHOCOLATE CREAM FILLING (page 141) for the other layer. Refrigerate the filling several hours or overnight. Spray two cookie sheets. Preheat oven to 450°.

NAPOLEON PASTRY DOUGH

Sift and mix DRY INGREDIENTS

DRY INGREDIENTS

☐	3 TBSP POTATO STARCH	☐	1 TBSP SUGAR
☐	1/3 cup RICE FLOUR	☐	1 tsp XANTHAN GUM
☐	1 tsp BAKING POWDER	☐	1/4 tsp SALT

Put SHORTENING MIX in a saucepan. Cook till it comes to a boil and the shortening is melted.

SHORTENING INGREDIENTS

☐ 1/2 cup WATER   ☐ 1/4 cup BUTTERY CRISCO

Add DRY INGREDIENTS to SHORTENING INGREDIENTS all at once. Stir with wooden spoon till blended. Add EGGS one at a time beating with an electric mixer after each addition.

☐ 2 EGGS

Place half the dough onto a sprayed cookie sheet. The dough will be sticky, so sprinkle with RICE FLOUR. Pat the dough into a 9" X 10" rectangle. Cut the dough in half, making two 5" strips. Do the same with the other half of the dough using the second cookie sheet. Bake at 450° for 15 minutes, or till toasty brown.

NAPOLEON

This recipe makes four Napoleons, each three layers high.
Use a sharp knife to trim and cut the baked pastry into 12
rectangles each 3" X 5".

TOP FROSTED LAYER

Spread four of the baked rectangles on a wire rack.
Mix the following ingredients till blended.

☐ **1 cup POWDERED SUGAR** ☐ **1 TBSP WATER**

Use a spatula to cover the four rectangles with the frosting.

Let the frosting set for a half hour, then melt the CHOCOLATE
INGREDIENTS in a microwave oven (Page 209).

CHOCOLATE INGREDIENTS

☐ **1 square SEMI-SWEET BAKING CHOCOLATE**
☐ **1 tsp BUTTER** ☐ **2 tsp HEAVY CREAM**

Drizzle the CHOCOLATE from a spoon in diagonal lines over the
frosting. Run the edge of a knife across the lines to give a ripple
effect (see picture page 168).

Assemble the NAPOLEONS.

BOTTOM LAYER

Top four baked rectangles with CREAM FILLING, using half of
the filling.

MIDDLE LAYER

Place a rectangle on top of the cream filling. Use the remaining
filling for the middle layer.

TOP FROSTED LAYER

Place the frosted rectangle on top of the cream filling.

Refrigerate for four or more hours and serve cold.

Deli Favorites

Raspberry Filled Cookie 183

Apple Crumb Cake 184

Black & White Cookie 186

Rugelach 188

Deli Marble Cake 190

Cheese Danish 192

Apple Strudel 194

Prune Pastry 196

RASPBERRY FILLED COOKIES

This Deli favorite is a cut-out cookie filled with raspberry preserves. There are cookie cutter kits on the market that make the special effects shown on the opposite page. Williams-Sonoma sells a fluted biscuit cutter set that will make different sized scalloped cookies. In the absence of these, make round cookies, fill with raspberry preserves and top with powdered sugar. They'll taste just as good.

Spray 2 cookie sheets. Preheat oven to 350°.
Follow the CUT-OUT COOKIE directions on page 50.

DRY INGREDIENTS
- ☐ 2/3 cup G-F CAKE FLOUR
- ☐ 1/2 tsp XANTHAN GUM
- ☐ 1/2 tsp BAKING POWDER
- ☐ 1/3 cup ALMOND MEAL
- ☐ 1/4 tsp SALT

SHORTENING INGREDIENTS
- ☐ 1/4 cup BUTTER
- ☐ 1/2 tsp ALMOND EXTRACT
- ☐ 3 TBSP SUGAR
- ☐ 2 TBSP MILK

Roll out the dough making twelve 3" bottom cookies and twelve decorative top cookies.

BAKING DIRECTIONS
Bake at 350° for 10 to 12 minutes or til slightly brown around the edge.

FILING
Place a teaspoon of the preserves on the bottom cookie.
- ☐ 1/3 cup RASPBERRY PRESERVES

Sprinkle the decorative top cookie with POWDERED SUGAR.
- ☐ 1/4 cup POWDERED SUGAR

Place the powdered decorative cookie on top of the JAM.

APPLE CRUMB CAKE

Apple Crumb Cake has a bottom crust that is more pie than cake, an apple filling and a crumb topping. It is baked commercially in large sheet pans and sold in rectangular pieces at the Deli. This is a recipe with large crumbs and thick apple filling — more generous than is usually sold.

Put the CRISCO in the freezer for at least a half hour before baking. Sliced apples tend to turn rusty so make the bottom crust and crumb topping before you begin to peel the apples.

Spray a square baking pan 8" X 8" X 2".

BOTTOM CRUST
Sift and mix DRY INGREDIENTS.
DRY INGREDIENTS
- ☐ 1 1/4 cup G-F ALL PURPOSE FLOUR
- ☐ 1 tsp BAKING POWDER
- ☐ 2 TBSP SUGAR
- ☐ 1 tsp XANTHAN GUM
- ☐ 1/2 tsp SALT

Cut SHORTENING into DRY INGREDIENTS (page 208).
SHORTENING   ☐ 1/3 cup CRISCO

Add LIQUID INGREDIENTS to form a pastry dough.
LIQUID INGREDIENTS
- ☐ 1/4 cup MILK   ☐ 1 EGG YOLK

Press dough into the bottom of the sprayed baking pan.
Use the back of a measuring cup to press the dough evenly on the bottom of the pan.

APPLE CRUMB CAKE

CRUMB TOPPING
Sift and mx TOPPING INGREDIENTS.

TOPPING INGREDIENTS
- ☐ 1 cup G-F ALL PURPOSE FLOUR
- ☐ 1/4 cup BROWN SUGAR
- ☐ 1/4 tsp CINNAMON
- ☐ 1/4 tsp salt
- ☐ 1/4 cup SUGAR
- ☐ 1/4 tsp NUTMEG

Cut BUTTER into the TOPPING INGREDIENTS.
- ☐ 5 TBSP BUTTER

Use your hands to form half inch to one inch crumbs, then set aside.

APPLE FILLING
Preheat the oven to 350⁰.

Peel and core 5 large APPLES. Use a food processor to thinly slice the APPLES. If you do not have a processor, slice the apples as thinly as you are able.
- ☐ 4 cups APPLES (Granny Smith or other tart apple)

Sprinkle APPLES with ORANGE JUICE
- ☐ 1 TBSP ORANGE JUICE

Mix the SUGAR INGREDIENTS and pour over the APPLES.

SUGAR INGREDIENTS
- ☐ 2/3 cup SUGAR
- ☐ 1 tsp CINNAMON

Put the APPLE FILLING over the BOTTOM CRUST.
Cover the filling with the CRUMB TOPPING.

BAKING DIRECTIONS
Bake AT 350⁰ for 45 to 50 minutes till apples are bubbly and the topping light brown. Sprinkle with POWDERED SUGAR and serve. It tastes best warm or at room temperature.
If you refrigerate the cake and it hardens, warm it in a microwave oven before serving.

BLACK & WHITE COOKIE

The Black & White Cookie has been a Deli favorite for as long as I remember (and that's long). The cookie is mixed like a cake and baked like a cookie. Frosting the Black & White Cookie takes time and a steady hand. That doesn't mean perfection. If a bit of chocolate spills over to the vanilla, or if the line separating them wavers, that's O.K. The cookie will still taste better than you remember.

Bring refrigerated ingredients room temperature (page 205). Spray two cookie sheets. Preheat oven to 350°.

Sift and mix DRY INGREDIENTS.
DRY INGREDIENTS
☐ 1 cup + 2 TBSP G-F CAKE FLOUR   ☐ 1/4 tsp SALT
☐ 1/2 tsp XANTHAN GUM   ☐ 1/2 tsp BAKING SODA

Mix LIQUID INGREDIENTS in a bowl and set aside.
LIQUID INGREDIENTS
☐ 6 TBSP BUTTERMILK   ☐ 1 tsp VANILLA

SHORTENING INGREDIENTS
Beat BUTTER and SUGAR with an electric mixer for 3 minutes.
☐ 1/3 cup BUTTER   ☐ 1/2 cup SUGAR
Add EGG and beat for another minute.
☐ 1 EGG

Alternate DRY and LIQUID INGREDIENTS into SHORTENING INGREDIENTS (page 57).

BAKING DIRECTIONS
Divide the batter evenly making 12 cookies (6 per cookie sheet). Leave room to spread. Bake at 350° for 15 - 18 minutes or till the top of the cookie is golden brown.
When room temperature, place on a wire rack and frost.

BLACK & WHITE COOKIE

Some bakeries frost the rounded top half of the cookie (as pictured on page 182). Other bakeries, turn the cookie upside-down and frost the flat side of the cookie. However you remember the cookie is the right way to frost it.

THE VANILLA HALF

Use a hand held electric mixer to beat the following ingredients together till smooth.

- ☐ 1 2/3 cups POWDERED SUGAR
- ☐ 1 TBSP LIGHT CORN SYRUP
- ☐ 1/2 tsp VANILLA
- ☐ 2 tsp LEMON JUICE
- ☐ 1 TBSP WATER

Use a butter knife to coat half of the cookies with VANILLA FROSTING. Start by making a straight line of frosting down the middle of the cookie. Spread the frosting outward to the edge of the cookie. Place on a wire rack.

THE CHOCOLATE HALF

Once you have frosted the white half of the cookie, there should be 2 to 4 tablespoons of VANILLA FROSTING left. Add the following ingredients to the left over frosting.

- ☐ 2 TBSP WATER
- ☐ 2 TBSP BAKING COCOA
- ☐ 1 cup POWDERED SUGAR

Beat with the electric beater until smooth.

Use a butter knife to coat the other half of the cookies with CHOCOLATE FROSTING.

Let dry at room temperature until the frosting hardens (about an hour).

RUGELACH

The spelling of this pastry varies depending on the locale. It can be spelled *Rugelakh* or *Ruggalach*, or as spelled above, *Rugelach*. Spelling may be questionable, but not the popularity of the pastry. It is right up front in the show case of delicatessens throughout the U.S.

Measure CRISCO and put in freezer an hour before baking.
Preheat oven to 350°. Spray two cookie sheets.
Measure out PRESERVES and set aside.
- ☐ 1 cup APRICOT PRESERVES (or ORANGE MARMALADE)

Stir the NUT MIXTURE with a spoon till blended. Set aside.
NUT MIXTURE
- ☐ 1/3 cup WALNUTS (chopped)
- ☐ 1/2 tsp CINNAMON
- ☐ 3 TBSP SUGAR
- ☐ 1/4 cup RAISINS

Stir the SUGAR MIXTURE with a spoon till blended. Set aside.
SUGAR MIXTURE
- ☐ 3 TBSP SUGAR
- ☐ 1/2 tsp CINNAMON

THE PASTRY

Sift and mix DRY INGREDIENTS.
DRY INGREDIENTS
- ☐ 1 1/3 G-F ALL PURPOSE FLOUR
- ☐ 1 tsp XANTHAN GUM
- ☐ 1/2 tsp SALT

Cut SHORTENING into DRY INGREDIENTS (page 208).
SHORTENING INGREDIENTS
- ☐ 3 TBSP BUTTER
- ☐ 1/4 cup CRISCO

Add LIQUID INGREDIENTS to form a smooth ball of dough.
LIQUID INGREDIENTS
- ☐ 1 1/2 tsp WHITE VINEGAR
- ☐ 1 1/2 tsp EGG SUBSTITUTE
- ☐ 2 TBSP WATER (ice cold)

RUGELACH

Divide the dough into 4 equal balls.
Roll one of the balls into a 7" circle.
Spread with 1/4 cup of PRESERVES out to a half inch of the edge.
Sprinkle with 3 tablespoons of the NUT MIXTURE.
Cut the circle into quarters.

There are two ways to roll the dough.
Pointy side out — start at the wide side of the triangle and roll inward (pictured on page 182).
Pointy side in — start at the point and roll outward (this method is easier to roll and covers most of the filling).
The right way, is the way you want to roll it.

Place the rolled pastry on a cookie sheets.
Turn the ends in slightly to form a crescent.

Role and fill with the remaining 3 balls of dough.
The recipe makes 16 Rugelach, 8 per cookie sheet.

Brush each pastry with EGG SUBSTITUTE.

☐ 1 TBSP EGG SUBSTITUTE

Sprinkle each pastry with rounded half a teaspoon of the SUGAR MIXTURE.

BAKING DIRECTIONS
Bake at 350° for 25 to 30 minutes or till golden brown.

DELI MARBLE CAKE

The Deli Marble Cake is a marbled sponge cake. It is so popular that restaurants set out complimentary squares at each table. It is the perfect companion to a hot beverage.

Beat EGGS with the whisk attachment of an electric mixer. When frothy, add CREAM OF TARTAR and beat for 15 minutes.
- ☐ 4 EGGS (room temperature)
- ☐ 1/2 tsp CREAM OF TARTAR

Gradually beat in SUGAR and VANILLA.
- ☐ 3/4 cup. SUGAR   ☐ 1 tsp VANILLA

Continue to beat for another 5 minutes.

Meanwhile, sift and mix the DRY INGREDIENTS.

DRY INGREDIENTS
- ☐ 1 1/4 cup G-F CAKE FLOUR   ☐ 1/4 tsp SALT
- ☐ 2 tsp BAKING POWDER   ☐ 1 tsp XANTHAN GUM

CHOCOLATE INGREDIENTS
- ☐ 1 square SEMI-SWEET BAKING CHOCOLATE

Melt the CHOCOLATE a small mixing bowl in a microwave oven. Add the following ingredients to the melted CHOCOLATE.
- ☐ 2 TBSP BAKING COCOA
- ☐ 1 TBSP LIGHT OLIVE OIL   ☐ 1 TBSP SUGAR

Stir till blended and set aside.

Preheat oven to 350°. Set aside a square baking dish 8" X 8" X 2" (do not spray or grease).

VANILLA BATTER
Heat MILK in a small saucepan till it bubbles around the edge.
- ☐ 1 cup MILK (whole milk or 2% fat)

Fold sifted DRY INGREDIENTS into beaten EGG MIXTURE. Fold the heated MILK into the batter until well blended.

DELI MARBLE CAKE

BAKING COCOA INGREDIENTS
- ☐ 2 TBSP BAKING COCOA
- ☐ 1 TBSP POWDERED SUGAR

Mix the COCOA and SUGAR in a small bowl and set aside.

CHOCOLATE LAYER
Stir 1 cup of the VANILLA BATTER into the melted CHOCOLATE INGREDIENTS until well blended.

Spread on the bottom of a square baking dish.

VANILLA LAYER
Spread a <u>thin</u> layer of the VANILLA BATTER on top of the CHOCOLATE LAYER.

BAKING COCOA LAYER
Use a metal strainer to sprinkle half the BAKING COCOA INGREDIENTS on top of the VANILLA LAYER.

2nd VANILLA LAYER
Pour half of the remaining batter on top of the BAKING COCOA layer.

2nd BAKING COCOA LAYER
Sprinkle the rest of the BAKING COCOA top of the VANILLA layer.

Top VANILLA LAYER
Top the second layer of COCOA with the rest of the batter.

Use a butter knife, held at an angle to marble. Cut down through the bottom chocolate layer in 3 circles and 5 straight lines.

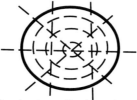

Bake @ 350° for 20 minutes. Reduce heat to 325° and continue baking for another 25 minutes or till cake is golden brown and begins to pull away from the sides of the pan. Let cake cool in the baking pan. Sprinkle with POWDERED SUGAR and serve.

CHEESE DANISH

Making a Cheese Danish takes time. The batter is mixed, then refrigerated. The next day, the dough needs to rise and then bake. A bit of an effort, but well worth it.

Sift and mix the DRY INGREDIENTS.
DRY INGREDIENTS
- ☐ 1 1/3 cup G-F ALL PURPOSE FLOUR
- ☐ 1 tsp XANTHAN GUM
- ☐ 3/4 tsp SALT
- ☐ 3 TBSP SUGAR

Cut BUTTER into DRY INGREDIENTS (page 208).
BUTTER
- ☐ 7 TBSP COLD BUTTER

Beat LIQUID INGREDIENTS with a fork until blended.
LIQUID INGREDIENTS
- ☐ 1 EGG
- ☐ 1 TBSP MILK

Pour the LIQUID INGREDIENTS into the batter and mix with a large spoon until blended. Cover the dough with plastic wrap and refrigerate overnight.

THE NEXT DAY
Spray two cookies sheets.
Sprinkle the YEAST and then the SUGAR on top of the WATER.
YEAST INGREDIENTS
- ☐ 2 TBSP WATER (luke-warm)
- ☐ 2 tsp YEAST
- ☐ 1 tsp SUGAR

Set aside a few minutes, stirring once or twice, until bubbly.

Remove the dough from the refrigerator. Break it into pieces in a mixing bowl. Use your hands to work the YEAST INGREDIENTS into the dough until blended. Divide the dough in half.
Make six pastries per half.

CHEESE DANISH

ROLLING THE DOUGH

ROUND   Use a round 4" cookie cutter or the 4" rim
              of a drinking glass to make round pastries.
SQUARE   Use a sharp knife to cut into squares, each 4" x 4".
See picture of round and square Cheese Danish (page 182).

Roll the dough using ROLLING DIRECTIONS given on page 50.
Place six pastries on each sprayed cookie sheet. Cover the cookie
sheets with plastic wrap and let rise until the surface looks
bumpy (1 to 1 1/2 hours). Meanwhile, bring the refrigerated
CHEESE FILLING ingredients to room temperature.

Preheat the oven to 350°.
Brush the border of each pastry with beaten EGG WASH.
EGG WASH   ☐   1 EGG YOLK + 1 tsp WATER

CHEESE FILLING

Combine the following ingredients in an electric mixing bowl.
Use the paddle attachment on high speed. Beat until blended.

☐ 4 oz CREAM CHEESE	☐ 3 TBSP SUGAR
☐ 1 TBSP RICOTTA CHEESE	☐ 1 EGG YOLK
☐ 1/2 tsp LEMON RIND (page 211)	☐ 1/8 tsp SALT

Put one tablespoon of FILLING in the middle of each pastry.
Take two opposing ends (opposing corners, if square) and fold
the dough over the filling. Firmly overlap the ends so they will
not come apart while baking.

Once filled and folded, brush the top and sides with the
remaining EGG WASH.

BAKING DIRECTIONS

Bake at 350° for 20 minutes or until golden brown.

APPLE STRUDEL

This Hungarian dessert is made with thin pastry dough and fruit or cheese filling. The following recipe is for the most popular of the Deli Strudels, namely Apple Strudel.

STRUDEL PASTRY

Sift and mix DRY INGREDIENTS.
DRY INGREDIENTS

- ☐ 1/2 cup G-F CAKE FLOUR
- ☐ 1/4 tsp SALT
- ☐ 1 1/2 tsp XANTHAN GUM

Beat the EGG INGREDIENTS in a small bowl till blended.
EGG INGREDIENTS

- ☐ 1 EGG
- ☐ 1 TBSP LIGHT OLIVE OIL
- ☐ 1 1/2 TBSP WATER

Add the EGG INGREDIENT to the DRY INGREDIENTS.
Use your hands to work the dough into a smooth ball.

Sprinkle a silicone mat with RICE FLOUR and roll the dough as thin as you can get it without tearing the dough. Try to stretch the dough into a 15" square. If it turns out to be a 15" circle, (or 15" blob) that's close enough.

Brush the dough with BUTTER.

- ☐ 2 TBSP BUTTER

Spray one cookie sheet.
Preheat oven to 400°.
Make the APPLE FILLING.

APPLE STRUDEL

APPLE FILLING

RAISIN MIXTURE
- ☐ 1/4 cup BLANCHED ALMOND SLIVERS (chopped)
- ☐ 2 TBSP RAISINS

Mix the RAISINS and ALMONDS and set aside.

SUGAR MIXTURE
- ☐ 1/2 cup SUGAR ☐ 1 1/2 tsp CINNAMON

Mix the SUGAR and CINNAMON and set aside.

BREAD CRUMB MIXTURE
- ☐ 1/3 cup fine G-F BREAD CRUMBS ☐ 3 TBSP BUTTER

Lightly brown the BREAD CRUMBS in the BUTTER and set aside.

APPLE MIXTURE

Use a food processor to thinly slice 3 or 4 apples. Sprinkle the APPLES with ORANGE JUICE.
- ☐ 4 cups APPLES (Granny Smith or other tart apple)
- ☐ 2 TBSP ORANGE JUICE

Spread the APPLES over the Strudel dough. Top the APPLES with the three MIXTURES in the order given: RAISIN, SUGAR, BREAD CRUMB. Top the BREAD CRUMBS with MELTED BUTTER.
- ☐ 2 TBSP MELTED BUTTER

Roll the dough into a roll and place it on the sprayed sheet. Brush the top with melted BUTTER.
- ☐ 2 TBSP MELTED BUTTER

BAKING DIRECTIONS

Bake at 400° for 20 minutes.

Brush with a tablespoon of melted BUTTER and lower heat to 350°. Bake for another 10 minutes.

Brush with another tablespoon of melted BUTTER and sprinkle with SUGAR. ☐ 2 TBSP SUGAR

Continue to bake for another 10 minutes or till golden brown.

Sprinkle with POWDERED SUGAR and serve warm from the oven.

PRUNE PASTRY

Prune Pastry is another delicatessen favorite. You can always spot it in the show case. It looks like a three cornered hat (see picture page 182).

PRUNE FILLING

Grate the rind from a large ORANGE (page 211).

Mix the following in a small saucepan.

- ☐   1/2 cup PRUNES (pitted and chopped fine)
- ☐   2 TBSP HONEY   ☐   1/4 cup ORANGE JUICE
- ☐   1 tsp LEMON JUICE   ☐   1 TBSP SUGAR

Stir over medium heat until the filling comes to a boil and the juices are absorbed into the prune. Remove from heat and stir in ORANGE RIND.   ☐   1 tsp ORANGE RIND

Spray two cookie sheets. Preheat oven to 350°.

PASTRY

Sift and mix DRY INGREDIENTS.

DRY INGREDIENTS

- ☐   1 cup G-F ALL PURPOSE FLOUR
- ☐   2 tsp BAKING POWDER   ☐   1/2 tsp SALT
- ☐   3/4 tsp XANTHAN GUM   ☐   3 TBSP SUGAR

Cut BUTTER into DRY INGREDIENTS (page 208).

         ☐   1/4 cup BUTTER   (cold from refrigerator)

Add MILK to form a ball of dough.

         ☐   3 TBSP COLD MILK

Roll the dough the same as cut-out cookies (page 50). Use a 3" biscuit cutter to make 18 circles. Place 8 circles on each sprayed cookie sheet. Divide the filling among the 16 pastries (about a teaspoon for each). Curl over 3 sides forming a "three-cornered hat." Squeeze each corner so they won't bake open.

Brush the top and outside with EGG SUBSTITUTE.

         ☐   1 TBSP EGG SUBSTITUTE

BAKING DIRECTIONS

Bake at 350° for 15 to 20 minutes till edges are lightly brown.

Appendix Index

THE GLUTEN FREE BLEND

The key to gluten free (G-F) baking and cooking is to substitute grains which when blended look and taste like regular (wheat) flour. The following blends do the job.

G-F ALL PURPOSE FLOUR
- 2 cups WHITE RICE FLOUR
- 2 cups TAPIOCA FLOUR
- 1 cup WHITE SORGHUM FLOUR
- 1 cup POTATO STARCH FLOUR
- 1 cup GARBANZO & FAVA FLOUR

G-F CAKE FLOUR.
- 2 cups WHITE RICE FLOUR
- 2 cups TAPIOCA FLOUR
- 1 cup WHITE SORGHUM FLOUR
- 1 cup POTATO STARCH
- 1 cup CORN STARCH

BOB's RED MILL produces all of the above grains. You can purchase the grains directly from the company over the Internet or you can find them in the gluten free section of WHOLE FOODS, INC.

IT STARTS WITH GLUTEN FREE FLOUR

With the exception of 15 recipes (pages 47, 60, 62, 68, 72, 88, 100, 105, 141, 142, 170, 172, 176, 178, 180) all the recipes in this book start with G-F All Purpose Flour or G-F Cake Flour. As explained on page 8 you can use commercial G-F All Purpose Flour for most of the recipes in this book. As of our print date, commercial G-F Cake Flour is not on the market. If you wish to bake one of the recipes in this book calling for G-F Cake Flour, you need to mix a batch of G-F Cake Flour using the above recipe.

THE GLUTEN FREE BLEND

HOW TO MAKE THE G-F BLEND

Assemble the following items:

- ▸ A package of each of the flours in the blend recipe
- ▸ A large metal strainer
- ▸ A large mixing bowl
- ▸ A large serving size spoon
- ▸ A large (4 quart) covered container with a top wide enough for a measuring cup.

1. Place the metal strainer over the mixing bowl. Measure the amount of flour given in the blend recipe into the strainer, then sift.

2. Mix the sifted flour with a large spoon until blended.

3. Transfer the mixed blend into the covered container. As discussed in the Introduction, density is a problem with G-F flour, so it is important to incorporate as much air as possible into the blend. Aerate the flour by shaking the container and turning it sideways and upside-down several times.

STORING THE BLEND

If you plan to use the blend within a few weeks, store it in an air tight container at room temperature. If you don't expect to use it up within a couple of weeks, store it in the refrigerator or freezer.

STORING LEFT OVER GRAINS

See directions on the package for the way to store a particular type of gluten free grain once the package is opened.

Getting Started

Ever watch the cooking celebrities on the Food Channel? They make it look so simple and all in a half hour. Easy for them, not because they are good cooks (which they are) but because they are prepared. The celebrities know:

- what they are going to cook
- how to cook it
- what equipment they need
- what ingredients they will use

You can be just as great a cook if you follow their lead. It's all in the planning. Before beginning:

READ THE RECIPE THROUGH

If there are any unfamiliar terms, look them up in the HOW TO section of this Appendix.

ASSEMBLE THE EQUIPMENT

There is certain basic equipment you need in order to measure, mix, cut/chop and cook (see next page). With the exception of the counter top electric mixer, these items are inexpensive. You will need special baking pans (also inexpensive) depending upon whether you going to bake cookies, pies or cakes.

Most of us accumulate kitchen equipment as we go along — buying what we need, when we need it. Yard sales are a good way to build your inventory. With a hint to a loved one, birthdays, holidays, anniversaries are opportunities to add to your collection.

ASSEMBLE THE INGREDIENTS

The recipes in this book give the ingredients in the order they are needed in the recipe. If you assemble and measure your ingredients before you begin, you will be as professional as a Food Channel star.

EQUIPMENT

Basic Equipment

MEASURING TOOLS

▸ a set of measuring spoons (teaspoon, tablespoon, etc.)
A set of odd size spoons such as 1/2 TBSP, 1/8 tsp is
not necessary, but convenient to have.

▸ a set of individual measuring cups
(1/8 cup, 1/4 cup, 1/3 cup, 1/2 cup, 1 cup)

MIXING TOOLS

▸ a large metal spoon for mixing

▸ a rubber spatula for scrapping the bowl

▸ a set of mixing bowls. Stainless steel is better than glass.
It's not as heavy and won't break when dropped.

▸ a set of wooden spoons (small, medium, large)

▸ three sizes of strainer (small, medium, large)

▸ a citrus squeezer (manual or electric)

▸ a hand held electric mixer

▸ a counter top electric mixer. This is a pricy item.
If you don't have one, use a hand held mixer.

CUTTING/CHOPPING EQUIPMENT

▸ a wooden or plastic chopping block

▸ a blender
They come in small and large sizes. Either size is
relatively inexpensive.

▸ a food processor

You can use a sharp knife and nimble hand to cut and slice,
but a food processor does a better job. You will bless it the
first time you bake an apple pie. It will slice apples thinner,
more uniform, than you can — and in seconds.

EQUIPMENT

COOKING EQUIPMENT

▸ 1 set of saucepans (small and medium)

▸ a double boiler or an oven proof bowl that
   fits into one of your saucepans

▸ a kitchen timer

Telephones ring, children cry. It's easy to get distracted when you're baking. A kitchen timer will remind you that food needs attending. It is an inexpensive tool that has saved many a gingerbread man from being burned alive.

COOKIE & CAKE EQUIPMENT

▸ a mini cupcake pan

▸ 1 square baking pan 8″ X 8″ X 2″.
   Glass baking dishes work best.

▸ 1 side-less cookie sheet (i.e., a flat cookie sheet)

This makes the job easier when baking cut-out cookies.

▸ 2 cupcake pans

Commercial quality, aluminized steel, cupcake pans give the best results. They keep the bottom of the cupcake from burning and allow cupcakes to rise higher.

▸ 2 large cookie sheets

The cookie recipes require large cookie sheets. If you have medium sized cookie sheets, you will need an extra cookie sheet for the given recipe. Insulated cookie sheets keep the bottom of the cookie from baking too quickly. Cookie sheets made of stainless steel or aluminum work best.

All of the above items are available at Williams-Sonoma stores or at their web site.

EQUIPMENT

CAKE EQUIPMENT

▶ two 9″ cake pans

▶ three 8″ cake pans

▶ a Bundt pan

▶ an angel food cake pan

▶ a metal wire rack (the one that comes with a toaster oven will do).

DECORATING TOOLS

A pastry bag with different nozzles to make different shapes.

PIE EQUIPMENT

▶ 1 rolling pin

▶ 1 silicone sheet

▶ a manual pastry blender
   (a handle with 5 blades attached)

▶ a saw-toothed pastry wheel

A pastry wheel cuts dough into even, serrated rows. It is a handy tool that makes professional looking lattice crust.

▶ pie pans

Glass pie pans bake evenly and you can look at the bottom to see whether the crust is brown. Experiment with different size and depth pans. You may find the traditional 9″ pan is great for fruit pies. A smaller, deeper pie pan may make a better custard or cream pie.

▶ a silicone or metal pie crust edge protector

Unless you like burnt crusts, an edge protector is a must.

USING THE EQUIPMENT

I usually muddle through kitchen equipment thinking it designed for those of average intelligence. When all else fails, I read the instructions. For those as mechanically challenged as I, it may take several trials before becoming comfortable with a kitchen appliance or tool. Even something as simple as a cookie sheet takes time to get to know. Cookies bake faster on teflon. Cookies baked on an insulated metal (aluminum or stainless steel) sheet take longer to bake, however they bake evenly and are less likely to burn the bottom of the cookie.

The suggested time given in our recipes is for an insulated cookie sheet. If you are using a teflon cookie sheet, you may need to lower the given temperature, or reduce the time. Whichever cookie sheet you use, keep a close eye on the cookies the first few times you bake them.

Using A Double Boiler

The reason a recipe calls for a double boiler is to melt chocolate or to cook something over a low, indirect heat. Fill the bottom of your double boiler so that the top pan does not touch the water. Heat the water to simmering (small bubbles) before putting the top pan in place. The goal is to have the water hot — not boiling. For electric ranges, turn off the heat once the water simmers. The range will remain hot long enough to melt the chocolate.

If you don't have a double boiler, use any set of sauce pans that fit one into the other, or place an oven proof bowl over a pot of simmering water so that the bowl is not touching the water.

HOW TO

MEASURE INGREDIENTS

Baking requires precise measurement with a set of measuring spoons. 1 tsp means 1 <u>level</u> teaspoon.

1 TBSP means one <u>level</u> tablespoon.

SEPARATE EGG WHITES

Eggs are best separated cold from the refrigerator. When separating more than one egg, do so one at a time in a separate small bowl. This avoids the risk of getting a bit of yolk into a bowl of whites.

BRING INGREDIENTS TO ROOM TEMPERATURE

Telling you to set out an ingredient until it reaches room temperature is like telling you to cook a roast till its done. It doesn't say how long. Of course, the time varies depending upon the size and starting temperature of the ingredient and the room temperature itself. But in general, eggs, butter, and a cup of milk, take an hour to come to room temperature. An 8 oz package of cream cheese takes about an hour and a half. If you want to bake NOW, you can put an egg into a cup of warm water for a few minutes and that will bring it to room temperature. You can soften butter by giving it a few seconds in the micro. Milk can be warmed the same way.

PREHEAT THE OVEN

To preheat the oven is to turn it on to the temperature given in the recipe. The oven will signal when its built in thermometer hits that temperature. Problem is, oven temperatures are not always accurate. The actual temperature may be higher (or lower) than indicated, causing a cake to rise improperly, or cookies to burn. Check the accuracy of the oven with an inexpensive oven thermometer found in the kitchen equipment section of the supermarket.

HOW TO

PREPARE BAKING PANS

There are three ways to prepare a baking pan:

Line The Cake Pan With Parchment

Place cake pan, upside-down on a sheet of parchment paper. Use a sharp knife to outline the shape of the pan. Cut the paper using the outline. Place a few drops of water on the cake pan to anchor the paper. Recipes that call for a parchment lining have batters that should not touch a greased surface, so do not grease the sides of the pan.

Butter The Baking Pan

Spread room temperature butter (or margarine) on the bottom and sides of the pan. Take a tablespoon of rice flour and sprinkle it around the pan. Roll the pan around to coat the butter. Turn the pan upside-down and tap out any excess flour.

Spray The Baking Pan

Spraying the pan is the easiest method. Use a gluten free unflavored baking spray such as Canola Oil Cooking Spray to spray the bottom and sides of the cake pan.

TEMPER EGGS

Some recipes call for eggs to be added to a hot mixture, but adding eggs all once makes scrambled eggs. To blend the eggs into a hot mixture without cooking them, beat the eggs in a separate bowl till just mixed. Add the hot mixture to the beaten eggs a tablespoon at a time, beating after each addition. After several tablespoons, the eggs are sufficiently "acclimated" and can be poured into the hot mixture and cooked according to the recipe. The process of gradually heating the eggs is called *tempering*.

HOW TO

BEAT EGG WHITES

Egg whites beat to their greatest volume when they are at room temperature. It is important to have the bowl spotlessly clean. The smallest amount of grease will deflate their volume. Adding Cream of Tartar at the beginning, when the whites are foamy, will make them beat firmer. Beat the egg whites until they are stiff with pointed peaks. Don't beat beyond that or they will dry out.

FOLD IN

A recipe may call for the beaten eggs to be "folded in" the batter. This instruction is used to keep as much of the air in the beaten egg as possible. To fold in, use a broad rubber spatula with a downward, turning motion in a single direction (right to left, or left to right). Fold until blended.

CREAM

To cream is to mix with a spoon or electric mixer until the ingredients (usually shortening and sugar) are smooth. It is important to have the shortening at room temperature.

SIFT AND MIX

Sifting has a twofold purpose: to mix the dry ingredients and to aerate them, i.e., to mix air with the ingredients. Sifting is done by measuring the dry ingredients into a sieve and then shaking them through. Once sifted, take a large spoon and mix the ingredients until well blended.

HEAT MILK TO A SIMMER

Put the milk in a saucepan over medium or high heat. In a few minutes, small bubbles will form around the edge of the saucepan. At that point, the milk is simmering hot.

HOW TO

CUT SHORTENING INTO DRY INGREDIENTS

Once upon a time (not so long ago) bakers cut shortening into the flour by running two knives in opposite directions until the shortening was pea sized. That's still a good way to cut in shortening. Then along came the manual pastry blender — a handle with 5 blades attached. It can be purchased in supermarkets, department store, or over the Internet, only today's pastry blender has thick wires instead of blades.

Some bakers use the blade attachment to a food processor to cut shortening into flour. They put shortening and flour into the food processor. With a few pulses the shortening is blended into the flour. Knives, manual pastry blenders or food processor, the goal is the same: mix the shortening into the flour until the shortening is the size of tiny peas and the flour looks coarse.

KNOW WHEN CAKE IS BAKED

A cake is baked when it is light brown around the edge and pulls away from the side of the pan. Touching it in the middle does not leave an impression. A toothpick, inserted in the middle of the cake, will come out clean, i.e., without any batter stuck to it.

CUT A CAKE IN HALF HORIZONTALLY

To cut a cake in half horizontally, use a small knife to make a guide cut midway between the top and bottom. Then use a long, thin knife to cut through the cake.

DUST WITH POWDERED SUGAR OR COCOA

Put powdered sugar (or unsweetened cocoa powder) into a small metal sieve. Tap the sieve gently with a knife over the baked goods.

HOW TO

COOK SYRUP TO SOFT BALL STAGE

It's easy to do with a candy thermometer. Cook the syrup till the thermometer measures between 235^0 and 240^0. You can cook to a soft ball stage without a thermometer, but it takes thinking and looking. Heat the syrup to boiling, stirring with a metal spoon. Let a drop of syrup fall off of the spoon into a glass of cold water. A drop that holds its shape as it sinks to the bottom has reached the soft ball stage. Immediately remove from the heat.

USE A PASTRY BAG

When the consistency is right, a pastry bag is easy to use. The key word is *consistency*. If the frosting or batter is too thin, it will dribble out — if too thick, it will clog the tip. The proper consistency is that of whipped cream, so when mixing frosting, or batter, think WHIPPED CREAM. To fill the pastry bag, turn down the top of the bag and put your batter in as close to the nozzle as possible. Unfold the top of the bag and squeeze it (not the middle) to get the batter into the nozzle. If you do not have a pastry bag, you can substitute a sealable plastic bag and a metal or plastic nozzle. Cut a small tip at one end of the bottom of the bag and push the nozzle in for a tight fit. Put in the frosting, or batter, seal the bag, then squeeze down from the top.

MELT CHOCOLATE SQUARES

There are two ways to melt baking chocolate squares: use a double boiler (page 204) or use a microwave oven. In both cases, cut the chocolate squares into quarters so they will melt quickly. To melt in a micro, place the chocolate uncovered in a clean dry dish. Put heat on high for 30 seconds, then stir with a dry spoon. Continue heating and stirring every 30 seconds till melted.

HOW TO MAKE

WHIPPED CREAM

It doesn't take much beating time to make whipped cream, so a hand held electric mixer can do the job. Place the mixing bowl and the beaters in the freezer for half an hour.

WHIPPED CREAM RECIPE

Pour heavy (not regular) whipping cream into the chilled bowl. ☐ 1/2 pint (1 cup) HEAVY WHIPPING CREAM
Beat on high till the cream forms soft peaks.

Gradually add sugar and vanilla while continuing to beat.
☐ 1/3 cup SUGAR   ☐ 1/2 tsp VANILLA
Beat until the mounds hold their shape. Do not over-beat.

GLUTEN-FREE CEREAL CRUMBS

Gluten free cereals are available in health food stores, at Whole Foods, Inc. and over the Internet. Crispy rice cereal and corn flakes make good cereal crumbs. Half of each make a nice blend. Recipes in this book contain a measured amount of sugar, so avoid making crumbs with frosted or sweetened cereals.

Once a box of cereal is opened it absorbs moisture. If the cereal is not crispy, put it on a clean cookie sheet and bake at 300⁰ degrees for 5 or 10 minutes. Do not brown the cereal. Just bake enough to restore its crunch.

Use a blender or a food processor with blade attachment to make crumbs. If you don't have either of these, place the cereal into a large sealable plastic bag and use a rolling pin to roll the cereal into crumbs or pound the plastic bag with a kitchen mallet. Three cups of cereal will reduce down to approximately 1 cup of crumbs. Cereal crumbs store well in the freezer or refrigerator.

HOW TO MAKE

Rind (orange, lemon, lime)

There are different size grating planes on the market. Some give a very fine grated rind. Others give thick chunks of rind that can be used as zest. When a recipe calls for grated rind, use a fine grating plane.

GRATING THE RIND

Rinse and dry the fruit. Place your plane over a bowl. Scrape the skin of the fruit on the plane. Scrape off only the outer skin of the fruit — that's where all the oils and favors are. Remove the grated rind from the back of the plane. In general, two lemons make a teaspoon of grated rind; one large orange makes a teaspoon of rind.

Zest (lemon, orange)

Lemon, or orange zest is a very thin strip of the outer skin of the fruit. Zest is made with a hand held kitchen utensil. It has a handle and a single blade with a row of small cutting holes on the top. It is used much like a potato peeler. The fruit is held in one hand while pressure is applied to the skin with the cutting edge of the tool. As with rind, start with clean dry fruit and work over a bowl to catch the zest as it peels off.

Chocolate Shavings

Take a thick bar of chocolate. Any will do. Stand the bar upright at an angle over a large dish. Use a potato peeler or a cheese slicer to scrape down the shavings from the bar.

EQUIVALENT MEASURES

1 TBSP = 3 tsp
1/4 cup = 4 TBSP
1/3 cup = 5 TBSP + 1 tsp
1/2 of 1/3 cup = 2 TBSP + 2 tsp
1/2 cup = 8 TBSP
2/3 cup = 10 TBSP + 2 tsp
3/4 cup = 12 TBSP
7/8 cup = 14 TBSP
1 cup = 16 TBSP

LIQUID MEASUREMENTS
1 liquid oz = 2 TBSP
8 liquid oz = 1/2 pint or 1 cup
16 fluid oz = 1 pint or 2 cups
32 fluid oz = 1 quart or 4 cups

EGG MEASUREMENTS
All recipes require large eggs.
1 EGG YOLK = 1 TBSP
1 LARGE EGG WHITE = 2 TBSP + 1 tsp

ABBREVIATIONS

tsp = teaspoon or teaspoons
TBSP = tablespoon or tablespoons
oz = ounce or ounces
RFT = Reasonable Facsimile Thereof

SUBSTITUTIONS

MARGARINE FOR BUTTER (maybe)
Substituting margarine for butter in a recipe could be a problem. They are not the same. Their salt content and fat content differ. Tub margarine remains soft when refrigerated. Not so with butter. This is not a problem with all recipes, so where possible we indicated that margarine is a permissible substitution.
BUT NOT LIGHT MARGARINE Light margarine has a higher liquid content than regular margarine, so do not substitute light margarine for butter or for margarine.

SUGAR SUBSTITUTE FOR SUGAR
If sugar is a problem, try using sugar substitutes that are designed for baking. Most recipes in this book work fine using a sugar substitute.

We all run out of ingredients from time to time. Here are some substitutions.

BAKING POWDER
   1 tsp = 1/2 tsp CREAM OF TARTAR + 1/4 tsp BAKING SODA

BROWN SUGAR
   1 cup = 1 cup SUGAR + 2 TBSP MOLASSES

CORN SYRUP (light)
   1 cup = 1 cup SUGAR + 1/4 cup WATER

SOUR CREAM
   1 cup = PLAIN YOGURT 1 cup

GLOSSARY

ALMOND MEAL/FLOUR (G-F) Is made with blanched almonds that have been finely ground. It is produced by BOB'S RED MILL.

BROWN RICE FLOUR (G-F) is made from unpolished brown rice.

BUCKWHEAT (G-F) is not wheat but an Eurasian herb originating in Central Asia and Siberia. The hull (outer cover) of the seed is removed and the groat (inner part of the seed) is milled into grain. The Russian name for cooked buckwheat is KASHA .

CREAM OF TARTAR (G-F) is made from pressed grapes. It is a natural fruit acid. When combined with baking soda, it is used as a leavening (i.e., rising or lightening) agent. It is used to make egg whites beat firmer and hold up better when baking.

EGG REPLACER is a product designed to replace eggs in a recipe. Some brands of EGG REPLACER contain gluten. EGG REPLACER produced by ENER-G FOODS, INC. is gluten free and lactose free, It is made from Potato Starch, Tapioca Flour, Leavening, Cellulose Gum and Carbonate Gum.

FAVA FLOUR (G-F) is made from the Fava bean (a legume).

GARBANZO FLOUR (G-F) Garbanzo flour is made from chick peas. It is high in protein.

GARFAVA (G-F) is an abbreviation for a flour that is a combination of GARBANZO FLOUR and FAVA FLOUR manufactured by Bob's Red Mill.

MACE (G-F) is a spice made from the outer shell of the seed of the Nutmeg. Mace has the flavor of nutmeg, although not as strong. You can use Nutmeg in place of Mace.

GLOSSARY

NUTMEG (G-F) is a spice that is native to the Spice Island in East India.

POTATO STARCH (G-F) also known as POTATO STARCH FLOUR is made from cooked potatoes that are processed until only the starch remains. NOTE: This is very different from POTATO FLOUR.

POTATO FLOUR (G-F) is ground from the whole potato. It is used as a thickener.

QUINOA (G-F) pronounced keen-wa) is an ancient grain used by the Inca civilization of South America. TRADITIONAL QUINOA or WHOLE GRAIN QUINOA can be purchased in health food stores or over the Internet.

RICE BRAN (G-F) is the edible seed coating of rice. It is available in most health food stores and over the Internet.

RICE FLOUR (G-F) also known as WHITE RICE FLOUR is made from white rice. It is available in super markets and health food stores. NOTE: This is not the same as SWEET RICE FLOUR.

SORGHUM FLOUR (G-F) is made from sorghum grain. It is packaged as 'SWEET' WHITE SORGHUM FLOUR by BOB's RED MILL.

TAPIOCA FLOUR (G-F) is also known as TAPIOCA STARCH. It is made from the cassava plant. This flour is basic to gluten free baking.

TEFF (G-F) is made from small grain. It is a basic staple used for centuries by the highland Ethiopians.

XANTHAN GUM (G-F) is made from the shell of a small, inactive (harmless) bacterium. It has the ability to hold particles of food together and is used as a substitute for gluten in G-F baking.

Index

Ingredient Index

A

ALMOND   34
> Blanched 145
> Meal   38, 47, 105, 120, 145, 183, 192
> Slivered 37, 141

APPLE
> Canned   154
> Fresh   124, 185, 195
> Sauce 36

APRICOT PRESERVES   89, 188

B

BANANAS   65, 142
BLUEBERRIES 104, 128
> Canned 153

BROWN RICE FLOUR   38, 105
BUCKWHEAT FLOUR   105
BUTTERMILK   18, 62, 82, 85, 103, 104, 107, 108, 137

C

CANDIED FRUIT   90
CARROTS   80
CEREAL
> CORN FLAKES   210
> CRUMBS 119, 120, 210
> RICE CEREAL   210

CHERRIES
> Canned   153
> Frozen   83, 122
> Preserves 179

CHOCOLATE
    Chips   22, 27, 28, 43
    Pudding   141
    Semi-Sweet Baking   19, 40, 63, 85, 96
                        137, 178, 181, 190
    White Chocolate Chip   29
CITRON   100, 112
COCOA, Semi-Sweet Baking   27, 35, 39, 63, 66, 67, 82
        119, 141, 147, 150, 157, 160, 166, 172, 187, 190
COCONUT FLAKES, Sweetened   36, 60, 84, 138, 140, 161, 163
COFFEE GRANULES   35, 172
CONDENSED MILK, Sweetened   87, 132
COTTAGE CHEESE   23
CORN MEAL 103
CORN SYRUP
    Light   38, 40, 61, 156, 187
    Dark   135
CRANBERRIES, Dried   37, 107
CREAM
    Cheese   71, 95, 99, 123, 172, 193
    Heavy   19, 40, 65, 87, 95, 99
              132, 139-142, 169, 181
    Sour   99, 123, 172

D
DATES, DRIED 37

E
EGG WHITES
    Dried   49, 61, 147
    Extra   66, 70, 76, 78, 88, 99, 104, 108, 157, 159, 177
    Only   30, 47, 60, 61, 68, 87

EGG YOLKS
Extra   34, 35
Only   41, 48, 84, 96, 98, 132, 136
         140, 176, 184, 193, 196

EVAPORATED MILK   77, 84, 87, 107, 122, 125, 127-129, 134

F
FIGS   148
FRUIT
         Candied   90
         Dried   31, 37

G
GELATIN   40
GOLDEN RAISINS   103

H
HEAVY CREAM   19, 40, 65, 87, 95, 99, 132, 139-142, 169, 181
HONEY   36, 38, 48, 49, 119, 148

K
KEY LIME   132

L
LEMON
         Juice   23, 42, 65, 69, 72, 99, 122, 131, 153, 174, 196
         Rind   23, 42, 72, 100, 128, 131, 174
         Zest   23
LIME JUICE   132

M

MACADAMIA NUT   29
MANDARIN ORANGES   89
MARASCHINO CHERRIES   77, 78, 169
MARSHMALLOW
    Cream   151
    Fluff 63
MASAREPA   103
MINI CHOCOLATE CHIP   27
MINUTE TAPIOCA   122, 129
MOLASSES   20, 53

N

NUTS   31, 35
    Almond   34, 37, 141, 145
    Macadamia   29
    Pecans   30, 77, 84, 111, 135
    Walnuts   21, 37, 43, 71, 80, 90, 106, 110

O

OATS, ROLLED   21, 36, 146

ORANGE
    Juice 65, 88, 89, 124, 148, 153, 154, 195, 196
    Mandarin   89
    Marmalade 188
    Rind   88, 100, 103, 104, 107, 129, 148, 196
    Zest   89

P

PEACHES   126

A Note From The Author

This book is the first in a series of three books. The title and abridged table of contents of the second book are:

Gluten Free Bread, Breakfast & Family Meals

BREAD	Basic Bread	Regional Bread
	Sweet Bread	Rolls & Biscuits

BREAKFAST	Pancakes & Waffles	Brunch
	Breakfast Bread (Bagels, English Muffin)	

SNACKS	Pretzels	Crackers
	Fair Favorites (corn dogs, funnel cakes)	

FAMILY MEALS	Appetizer	Soup
	Pasta	Main Course

NO BAKE DESSERTS	Doughnuts (raised & cake)	
	Ice Cream Treats	Cobblers

The book is scheduled for release in the middle of 2011.

I don't have a table of contents for the third book in this series of gluten free books. The tentative title is:

New Recipes For The Gluten Free Diet

It will contain original recipes I developed while writing the first two books.

I tried to include all of the popular desserts I could think of in this first gluten free book. If I missed one of your favorite desserts, please let me know via e-mail:

info@eaglepublishing.com

and I will try to include a recipe for that dessert in the third book of the series.